FOREST

PHOTOGRAPHED BY
FRANK GREENAWAY
KIM TAYLOR & JANE BURTON

WRITTEN BY
THERESA GREENAWAY
CHRISTIANE GUNZI
& BARBARA TAYLOR

DK

DK

A DK PUBLISHING BOOK

Project editor Christiane Gunzi
Art editors Floyd Sayers, Val Cunliffe
Editors Deborah Murrell, Sue Copsey
Editorial assistance Alexandra Tinley, Jill Somerscales
Illustrations Nick Hall, Nick Hewetson, Dan Wright
Production Samantha Larmour, Louise Barratt
U.S. Assistant editor Camela Decaire
Index Jane Parker

Natural history consultants
Geoff Boxshall, Barry Clarke, Andy Currant,
Theresa Greenaway, Paul Hillyard, Gordon Howes,
Judith Marshall, Tim Parmenter, Paul Pearce-Kelly,
Mark O'Shea, Matthew Robertson,
Edward Wade, Karen Willson

Picture credits
Bruce Coleman Ltd/Erwin & Peggy Bauer: 9t;/Gerald Cubitt: 10bc;
Hutchison Library: 8c;/Goylolea: 8br;/P.E. Parker : 46-47; **Image Bank**/
W. von dem Bussche: 9c;/Ross M. Horowitz: 46tc **NHPA**/George Gainsburgh: 10-11;
Premaphotos Wildlife/K.G. Preston-Mafham:81; **Tony Stone**/Sue Cunningham: 8bc;
Survival Anglia Ltd/Nigel Westwood: 9r; **Jerry Young**: 11tc, tr, 47tc

First American Edition, 1994
4 6 8 10 9 7 5 3
Published in the United States by
DK Publishing, Inc.,
95 Madison Avenue, New York, New York 10016

ISBN 1-56458-669-3

Color reproduction by Colourscan, Singapore
Printed and bound in Italy by New Interlitho, Milan

CONTENTS

FORESTS OF THE WORLD

Cuvier's toucan

FIVE THOUSAND YEARS ago, more than half the Earth was covered with forests. Today, forests cover about one third of the land. Forests are important for many reasons. They provide food and shelter for animals and plants, help prevent soil erosion, and play a vital role in climate control. There are several kinds of forests, depending on their geographical location and climate. All the plants and animals in this book live in tropical or temperate forests.

Madagascar periwinkle

MEDICINAL PLANTS
Many of the important medicines we use are produced from plants that grow in rain forests. This Madagascar periwinkle is used to make a drug to treat some kinds of cancer.

Mangrove snake

TROPICAL FORESTS
Close to the Equator, where the climate is warm all year, there are tropical rain forests. This is where trees such as teak and mahogany grow. In areas with distinct dry and rainy seasons, there are tropical seasonal forests.

Types of forest
Boreal
Temperate
Tropical
Tropical seasonal
Mangrove

FOREST PEOPLES
People have lived in harmony with forests for thousands of years, and in some parts of the world they still do. Rain forest peoples grow a mixture of vegetables and other crops, then leave the soil to recover. In this way, they make the best use of the land.

The largest rain forest is in the Amazon River Basin in South America.

Day gecko

DEFORESTATION
Rain forests are decreasing in size as thousands of trees are felled each year for timber and to make space for building. A forest takes hundreds of years to recover. Scientists believe that deforestation in rain forest areas may cause permanent changes in the Earth's climate.

Tiger centipede

A huge building site in the rain forest

MANGROVE FORESTS
Along the coasts of tropical areas are swampy mangrove forests. Mangrove trees are the only trees that can grow in salt water, and their large tangled roots are strong enough to survive flooding. Animals such as crocodiles and water snakes live here.

Mangrove roots

CONSERVATION

All kinds of animals and plants are endangered due to habitat loss. In rain forests about a dozen species become extinct every day. In temperate forests, several mammals are rare, in part because they have been hunted for their fur. Some countries' forests have been made national parks in order to help preserve the environment and its wildlife.

Comma butterfly

The biggest area of forest stretches in a band about 3,600 miles (5,800 km) long.

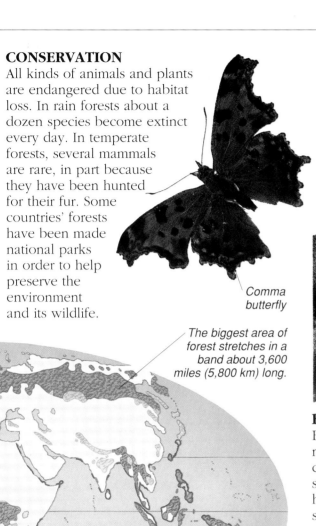

Mangroves grow along the coasts near tropical forests.

TEMPERATE FORESTS

These forests grow in temperate regions north and south of the Equator. In the north, they contain deciduous trees and some conifers. In the south, they contain evergreen broadleaved trees and conifers. Deciduous trees lose their leaves in autumn and grow new ones in spring. Evergreen trees keep their leaves all year.

BOREAL FORESTS

Boreal forests are found in the far north where winters are extremely cold and the growing season is short. The trees in a boreal forest have a conical shape that allows snow to slide off branches.

FOREST PRODUCTS

Forests supply us with many important products. Wood from the trees is made into paper, plywood, fuel, furniture, and many other things. In addition to supplying us with wood, forests provide oils, gum, cork, latex for making rubber, cinnamon, maple syrup, rayon, acetate, and other fibers.

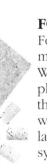

Cinnamon stick

Cork

Green woodpecker

MANAGING THE FORESTS

The trees in a forest need to be looked after so that the forest stays healthy. Forestry is concerned with managing forest areas and controlling timber use so as not to damage the environment. New trees are planted to replace felled ones, and young trees are carefully tended and protected from animals that may eat them.

Gray squirrel

Common weasel

TROPICAL RAIN FORESTS

THE RICHEST VARIETY of wildlife on Earth is found in tropical rain forests around the Equator. There are so many millions of plant and animal species living here that most of the invertebrates are yet to be discovered. Tropical rain forests are damp, warm places, with up to 160 in (4 m) of rain each year. Some tropical trees grow to great heights and form a protective canopy over the forest floor. They provide shelter and food for more than half the animal and plant species in the world.

Many rain forest trees have pointed leaves. Rainwater drips off the tip without damaging the leaf.

AIR PLANTS

Some of the common plants in a rain forest are epiphytes such as bromeliads. Epiphytes grow on trees and other plants without harming them. They are also called "air plants" because they get most of their water from moisture in the air.

A bromeliad traps water inside its leaves.

FRUITS AND NUTS

It is not only birds that eat rain forest fruits and seeds. Brazil nuts are collected from the rain forest, and so are many of the fruits that we buy, including passion fruit and kiwano (horned melon).

Kiwanos

Brazil nuts

LAYERS OF A TROPICAL FOREST

A tropical forest consists of layers. The understory layer contains plants from 16-40 ft (5-15 m) tall. Above is the canopy, where trees grow up to 60-90 ft (20-30 m). The emergent layer consists of a few trees measuring about 130 ft (40 m).

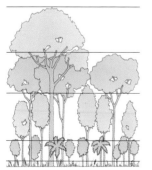

Emergent trees

Canopy layer

Herb layer

Understory Forest floor

BUTTRESS ROOTS

Many rain forest trees have developed huge roots that fan out at the base of the tree trunk. These wide "buttress" roots act like stabilizers, supporting the tall trees so that they do not topple over.

Buttress roots of a rain forest tree

INSECTS

There are more insects in a rain forest than any other kind of animal. Many insects are camouflaged so that they look like leaves or flowers. This helps them hide from predators.

Leaf insect

MAMMALS

Some kinds of monkeys have developed prehensile tails and grasping hands. These help them to hold on as they climb and swing through the branches of tall rain forest trees.

Black spider monkey

BIRDS

Birds are among the most brightly colored rain forest animals of all. This Fire-tufted barbet lives in dense forested areas, where it feeds on tropical fruits.

Fire-tufted barbet

Poison arrow frogs

AMPHIBIANS

Many rain forest amphibians are tree dwellers. Some, such as these poison arrow frogs, have poison glands in their skin. Their bright coloring warns birds and other animals to leave them alone because they taste horrible.

Rainwater that the trees do not absorb evaporates into the atmosphere.

RAIN FOREST RECYCLING

Many forest soils are very ancient so they are low in nutrients. In a tropical forest, where the climate is moist and warm, trees absorb and recycle rainwater and nutrients very quickly. This means that the soil in a rain forest is often poor, because the trees use most of the soil's nutrients as they grow.

Throughout the day, trees constantly take in and give out oxygen and carbon dioxide during respiration and photosynthesis.

Rotten fruits, leaves, and dead animals fall to the ground, where they are recycled by animals, bacteria, and fungi.

Leaf litter, dead plants, and fallen fruits do not remain on the forest floor for long. It is so warm and moist that everything rots away very quickly.

RAINBOW BIRD

THIS CUVIER'S TOUCAN hops through branches of tall rain forest trees. It uses its long bill to reach berries and seeds on twigs that are too thin for it to perch on. By tossing back its head, it can flick food down its throat. Toucans are sociable birds and live in flocks, sometimes preening other toucans or offering them food. They also play games, such as throwing fruit to each other. Toucans do not build nests. Instead, they live in holes in tree trunks. Females lay as many as four white eggs and both parents share the task of keeping the eggs warm. When young toucans hatch, they are blind. Their feathers do not start to grow until they are nearly four weeks old. At about six weeks old, they have enough feathers to learn to fly and leave the nesting hole.

WAVING THE FLAG
The toucan uses its brightly colored bill like a flag to signal to other toucans. The colors help it locate birds of its own kind and find a mate. Sometimes toucans use their bills to frighten off smaller birds, so that they can steal other birds' eggs and young.

The large bill looks heavy, but actually it is hollow and light.

Each toucan's bill is slightly different in color and pattern. This helps individual birds recognize each other.

Passion fruit is one of the toucan's favorite foods. Its bright color makes it easy to find.

Serrated (notched) edges on the bill allow the toucan to bite off chunks of fruit.

When sleeping, the toucan lays its huge bill on top of its back and covers it with its tail.

FACT FILE
Name Cuvier's toucan
(*Ramphastos cuvieri*)
Size Beak 5 in (13 cm) long
Distribution South America

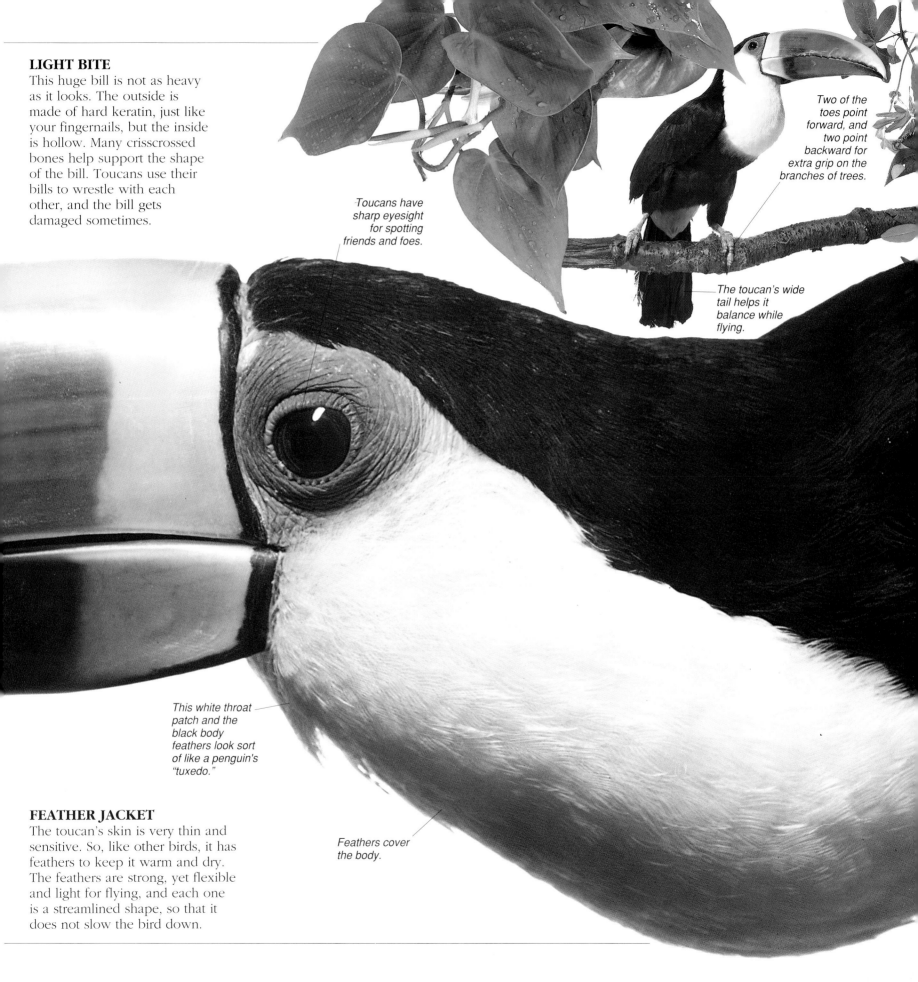

LIGHT BITE

This huge bill is not as heavy as it looks. The outside is made of hard keratin, just like your fingernails, but the inside is hollow. Many crisscrossed bones help support the shape of the bill. Toucans use their bills to wrestle with each other, and the bill gets damaged sometimes.

Toucans have sharp eyesight for spotting friends and foes.

Two of the toes point forward, and two point backward for extra grip on the branches of trees.

The toucan's wide tail helps it balance while flying.

This white throat patch and the black body feathers look sort of like a penguin's "tuxedo."

FEATHER JACKET

The toucan's skin is very thin and sensitive. So, like other birds, it has feathers to keep it warm and dry. The feathers are strong, yet flexible and light for flying, and each one is a streamlined shape, so that it does not slow the bird down.

Feathers cover the body.

HAIRY HUNTER

THIS LARGE, HAIRY SPIDER is not as dangerous as it looks. The curly-haired tarantula can kill small rodents, reptiles, or birds, but its bite is usually no more dangerous to people than a bee or wasp sting. During the day, tarantulas lurk under stones, bark, or leaves, or inside their silk-lined burrows on the forest floor. At night, they come out to hunt. Curly-haired tarantulas feel for prey in the darkness with the two leglike pedipalps on the front of the body. Female tarantulas lay eggs, then cover them with a cocoon of silk for protection. The young spiderlings hatch inside the cocoon and emerge after they have molted (shed their skins) once. As they grow into adults, they molt several more times. Female tarantulas, like this one, also molt when they are adults.

Spinnerets at the end of the abdomen (rear part of the body) produce silk.

Each hair is shaped like a tiny harpoon. The hooks along the sides cause itching and sneezing.

ITCHY HAIRS
The hairs on the tarantula's body sense vibrations in the air. This helps the spider find its way around and hunt in the dark. The hairs on its abdomen break off easily and irritate the skin of other animals, including humans. Tarantulas use their back legs to flick these hairs at enemies.

SPINNING SILK
At the end of the abdomen, there are four spinnerets that the spider uses to spin silk. The silk is stronger than the same thickness of nylon rope or steel cable, and it is very stretchy.

FACT FILE
Name Curly-haired tarantula
(*Brachypelma albopilosa*)
Size 3.5 in (9 cm) across
Distribution South America

The body consists of two parts with a narrow waist, called a pedicel in the middle.

Each leg is made up of seven parts, with two claws at the end and a tuft of hair underneath for extra grip.

POISON FANGS

Tarantulas are strong spiders. They pounce on their prey and hold it still with their pedipalps while their fangs inject poison. The poison paralyzes the prey and a special fluid from the spider's stomach digests the soft parts. The spider then sucks up the contents of its victim's body.

The eight simple eyes are tiny, so the spider has poor eyesight.

Pedipalps look like extra legs.

Huge fangs inject prey with poison.

MINI MONKEYS

HIGH UP IN THE CANOPY of the forest, families of little marmosets scurry along the branches, twittering to each other in soft voices. Although marmosets are monkeys, they behave much like squirrels. They run and leap from branch to branch and sit nibbling fruits, which they hold in their front paws. Marmosets need to be very sure-footed in their treetop home, so they have sharp claws for gripping branches. They eat fruits and leaves, as well as small animals such as young birds, tree frogs, lizards, and insects. They are also fond of the sweet, gummy sap that oozes out of damaged trees. Sometimes they deliberately cut into a tree to make the sap flow. Marmosets are active during the daytime. At night, they hide away in tree holes, which give them shelter and protection.

Thick, well-groomed fur keeps the animal dry. The adults' fur is long enough for the young to cling on to for safety.

FAMILY MATTERS

There are usually between three and eight marmosets in a family group. There are two adult parents, and several youngsters. The adult males help care for their young, often carrying them around in the treetops.

FACT FILE
Name Common marmoset
(Callithrix jacchus)
Size Body 9 in (23 cm) long
Distribution Brazil

The marmoset grips food in its front paws.

All common marmosets have these ear tufts of long white fur.

LAPPING SAP

In order to make sap dribble out of a tree trunk, marmosets have to cut through the bark and into the living wood. They do this by biting into the tree with their top incisors (front teeth). Then they gnaw upward with their lower incisors and lap up the sweet juice.

Marmosets have very good eyesight. Their large eyes can spot food from a long distance.

The nostrils open out on each side of the flat nose.

GROOMING IN GROUPS

Members of a family group spend a lot of time every day grooming one another. Grooming is important for marmosets. As well as getting rid of parasites and tangles in their fur, it also acts as a form of communication. It helps them make friends with one another, and to decide which animals are the leaders of the group.

Sharp claws help the marmoset run and jump from branch to branch without falling off.

The striped tail is longer than the body, and helps the marmoset balance.

LEAFY LIZARD

THIS MADAGASCAR DAY GECKO should be easy to spot. But, in fact, it is difficult to see, because it lives among the bright green forest leaves. As the name suggests, day geckos are active during the day. This is unusual, because most kinds of geckos come out only at night. Day geckos eat insects, fruit, and the sweet nectar from flowers. The female lays at least two clutches (batches) of eggs every year. There are only two eggs in each clutch. At first, the eggshells are sticky and soft. The gecko presses the eggs together and pushes them into a crack in tree bark. As the eggs dry, they harden and stick fast to the tree. The young hatch out after about nine weeks, breaking open their shells with a special egg tooth on the tip of the snout.

FACT FILE
Name Madagascar day gecko
(Phelsuma madagascariensis)
Size 6 in (16 cm) long
Distribution East Africa and Indian Ocean islands

These large, round eyes give the gecko very good color vision.

SKIN FOR SUPPER
The scaly skin of a lizard cannot stretch as the lizard grows. So from time to time, when the skin gets too tight, the lizard sheds it, to reveal a new one which has grown underneath. This is called sloughing. To remove the old skin, the lizard rubs itself against rough surfaces. Then it pulls off the old skin with its mouth and eats it.

After it has eaten, the gecko cleans its face and eyes with its long tongue.

This gecko cannot blink. Instead, each eye is protected by a transparent (clear) scale, called a brille.

Nostrils on the tip of the snout help the gecko find food.

These small, sharp teeth grip and crunch up food, such as insects.

ACROBATICS
Geckos are very agile. They can run along the undersides of branches upside down. Geckos can grip so well because they have tiny bristles on the undersides of their toes which can grasp even the tiniest bumps.

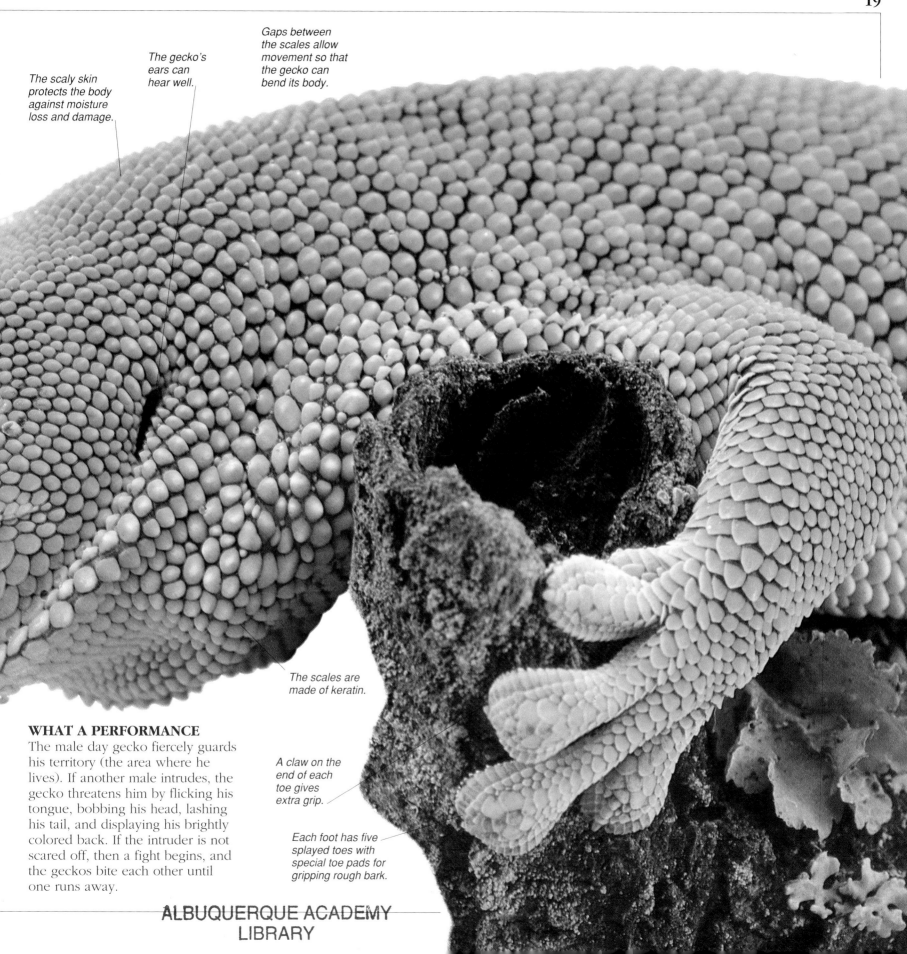

The scaly skin protects the body against moisture loss and damage.

The gecko's ears can hear well.

Gaps between the scales allow movement so that the gecko can bend its body.

The scales are made of keratin.

A claw on the end of each toe gives extra grip.

Each foot has five splayed toes with special toe pads for gripping rough bark.

WHAT A PERFORMANCE

The male day gecko fiercely guards his territory (the area where he lives). If another male intrudes, the gecko threatens him by flicking his tongue, bobbing his head, lashing his tail, and displaying his brightly colored back. If the intruder is not scared off, then a fight begins, and the geckos bite each other until one runs away.

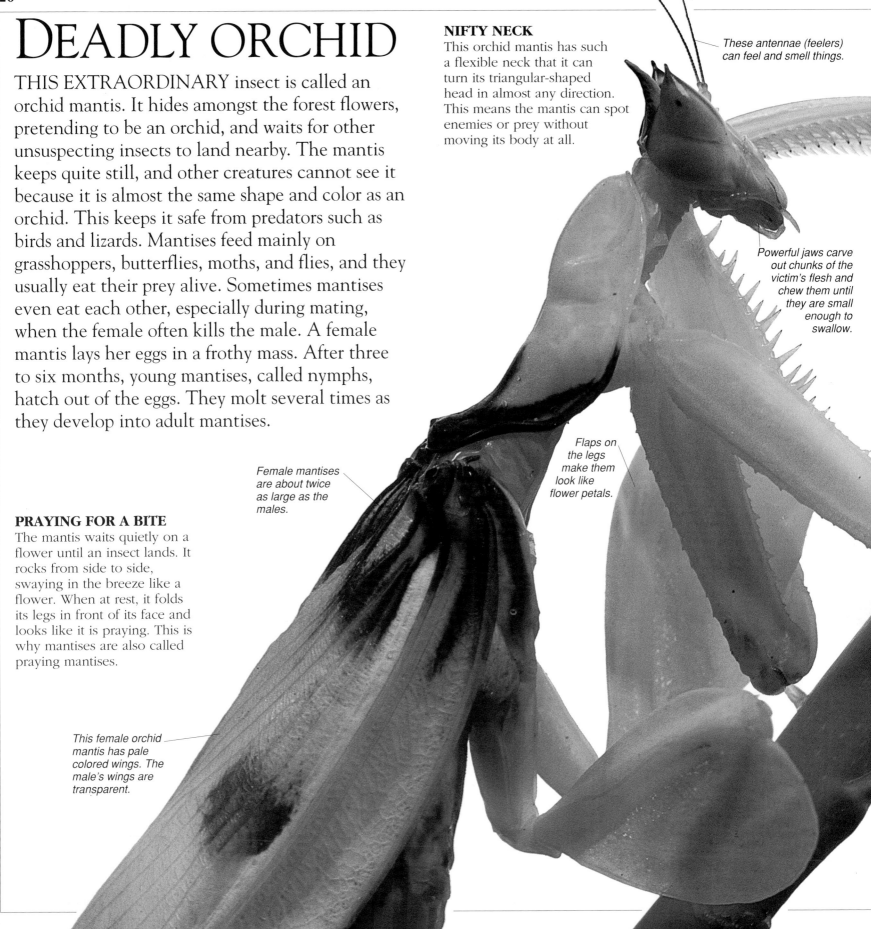

DEADLY ORCHID

THIS EXTRAORDINARY insect is called an orchid mantis. It hides amongst the forest flowers, pretending to be an orchid, and waits for other unsuspecting insects to land nearby. The mantis keeps quite still, and other creatures cannot see it because it is almost the same shape and color as an orchid. This keeps it safe from predators such as birds and lizards. Mantises feed mainly on grasshoppers, butterflies, moths, and flies, and they usually eat their prey alive. Sometimes mantises even eat each other, especially during mating, when the female often kills the male. A female mantis lays her eggs in a frothy mass. After three to six months, young mantises, called nymphs, hatch out of the eggs. They molt several times as they develop into adult mantises.

NIFTY NECK
This orchid mantis has such a flexible neck that it can turn its triangular-shaped head in almost any direction. This means the mantis can spot enemies or prey without moving its body at all.

These antennae (feelers) can feel and smell things.

Powerful jaws carve out chunks of the victim's flesh and chew them until they are small enough to swallow.

Flaps on the legs make them look like flower petals.

Female mantises are about twice as large as the males.

PRAYING FOR A BITE
The mantis waits quietly on a flower until an insect lands. It rocks from side to side, swaying in the breeze like a flower. When at rest, it folds its legs in front of its face and looks like it is praying. This is why mantises are also called praying mantises.

This female orchid mantis has pale colored wings. The male's wings are transparent.

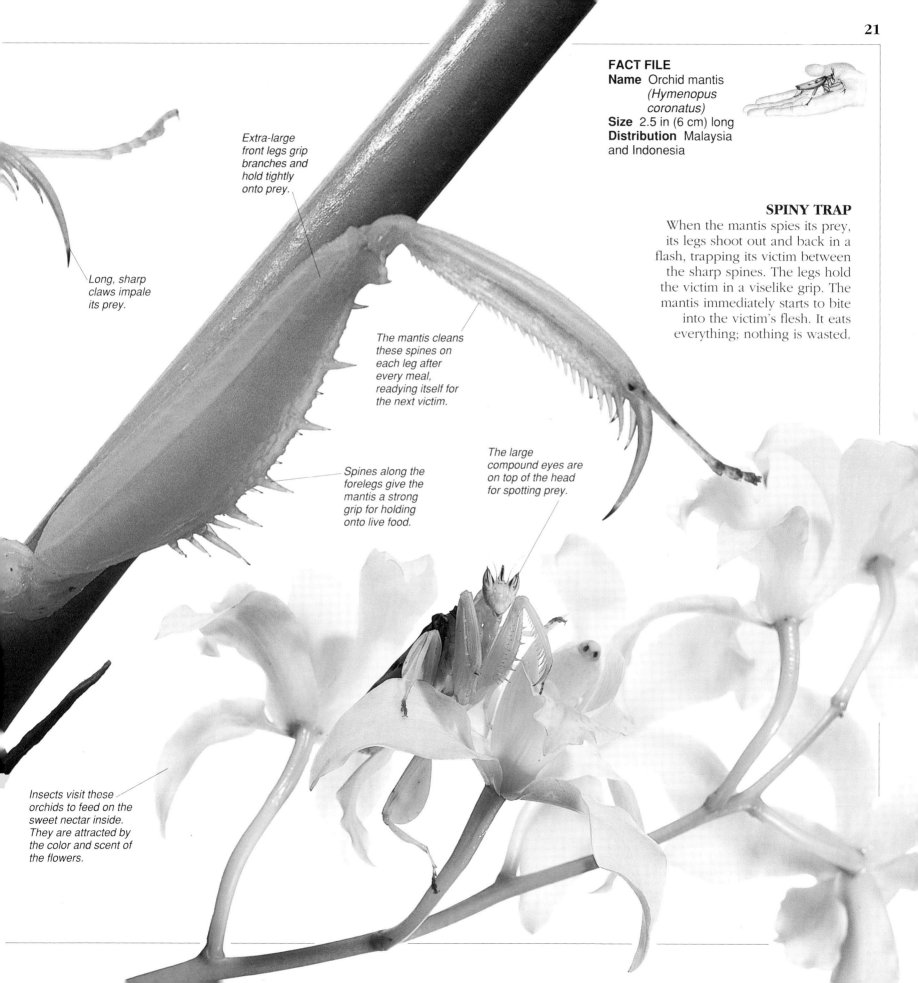

Long, sharp claws impale its prey.

Extra-large front legs grip branches and hold tightly onto prey.

FACT FILE
Name Orchid mantis
(Hymenopus coronatus)
Size 2.5 in (6 cm) long
Distribution Malaysia and Indonesia

SPINY TRAP
When the mantis spies its prey, its legs shoot out and back in a flash, trapping its victim between the sharp spines. The legs hold the victim in a viselike grip. The mantis immediately starts to bite into the victim's flesh. It eats everything; nothing is wasted.

The mantis cleans these spines on each leg after every meal, readying itself for the next victim.

Spines along the forelegs give the mantis a strong grip for holding onto live food.

The large compound eyes are on top of the head for spotting prey.

Insects visit these orchids to feed on the sweet nectar inside. They are attracted by the color and scent of the flowers.

BRILLIANT BUTTERFLIES

THESE BEAUTIFUL swallowtail butterflies flash in the sunlight as they fly among tropical trees. The male jealously guards his territory, chasing other males away. The female lays her eggs on the underside of a leaf. When the caterpillars hatch out, they are a brownish color. As they grow, they molt several times. Each time they molt, they become greener, until they are bright green. When the caterpillar is fully grown, it turns into a pupa. Its skin becomes hard, like a shell, and it does not move or eat for about two weeks. During this time many changes take place, until eventually the shell splits and a colorful butterfly emerges. This transformation is called metamorphosis.

NOW YOU SEE IT, NOW YOU DON'T
The bright colors on the upper surface of the wings are easily seen by enemies such as birds. So as soon as it lands, the swallowtail folds its wings together. The undersides of the wings are brown, so the butterfly blends in with the forest background, making it difficult to see.

SUGAR SUCKER
The swallowtail butterfly feeds on nectar. This is the sweet, sugary liquid produced by flowers. It uses its long, tubelike mouthpart, called a proboscis, to suck up the nectar, in the same way that you use a straw to suck up a drink.

These brownish colors help the swallowtail blend in with its surroundings.

The eyespots confuse predators, which mistake them for the butterfly's head.

The legs are long enough to hold the body clear of objects that might get in its way.

The abdomen contains the organs for reproduction and for digesting food.

FALSE EYES
The orange areas on the wings are called eyespots. They help protect the swallowtail by confusing its enemies, such as birds. They peck at an eyespot, mistaking it for the butterfly's head. So only the wings are damaged.

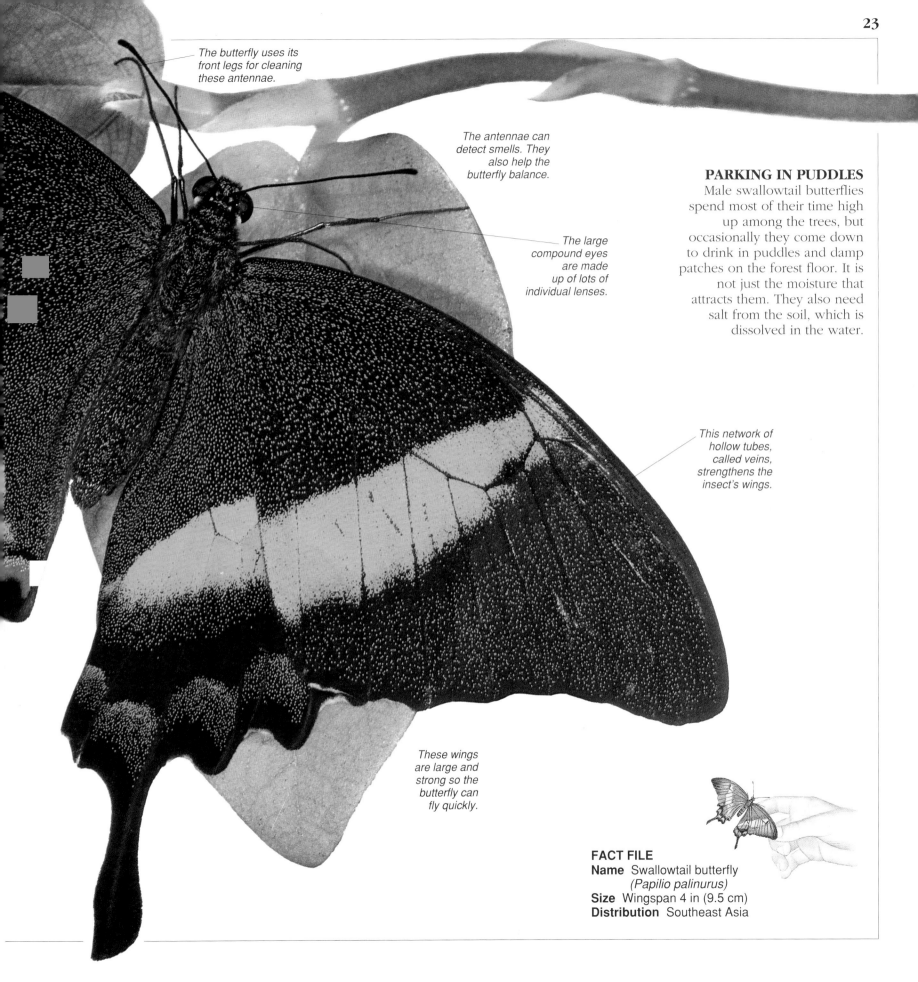

The butterfly uses its front legs for cleaning these antennae.

The antennae can detect smells. They also help the butterfly balance.

The large compound eyes are made up of lots of individual lenses.

PARKING IN PUDDLES

Male swallowtail butterflies spend most of their time high up among the trees, but occasionally they come down to drink in puddles and damp patches on the forest floor. It is not just the moisture that attracts them. They also need salt from the soil, which is dissolved in the water.

This network of hollow tubes, called veins, strengthens the insect's wings.

These wings are large and strong so the butterfly can fly quickly.

FACT FILE
Name Swallowtail butterfly
(*Papilio palinurus*)
Size Wingspan 4 in (9.5 cm)
Distribution Southeast Asia

GLIDING GECKO

THE FLYING GECKO lives high up in the trees. This lizard does not really fly, but its body has adapted so it can glide from tree to tree to escape danger. Flying geckos are active mainly at night, when it is cooler. Their excellent eyesight and hearing help them find insects to eat. Geckos lay one or two eggs that have soft, sticky shells. They often hide the fragile eggs under tree bark until the shells harden. The young geckos take several months to develop within their shells. Eventually, they break out by using the pointed egg tooth on their snout.

The eyes have a fixed, transparent covering. Most other lizards have movable eyelids.

These mottled colors camouflage the gecko against the bark and leaves in the forest.

A gecko clicks its tongue against the roof of its mouth when courting a mate or defending territory.

These flaps of skin act as parachutes when the gecko leaps from tree to tree.

If the tail is broken off, a new one slowly grows to replace it.

NIGHT SIGHT

The pupils of the eyes open wide to help the gecko see in the dark. In daylight, they close to a slit to protect the sensitive eyes from the light. The gecko cannot blink to clear its eyes, but wipes them clean with its tongue.

LEATHER PARACHUTE

Flaps of leathery skin along the sides of the gecko's body and tail can spread out like wings for gliding. This makes the lizard's body flatter and wider so it falls more slowly through the air. A parachute slows down a person's fall from an airplane in a similar way.

The gecko spreads its feet out as wide as possible for gliding.

Webbing between the toes helps the gecko steer as it glides.

Sharp claws and long toes cling to the bark of trees.

SCALY TOES

Each of the gecko's toes has a flat pad covered with ridges of scales. On these scales are many thousands of microscopic hairs that point backward. When the gecko presses its feet against a surface, the hairs stick in the cracks and pits, giving the lizard a gluelike grip.

Ridges of scales under the feet enable the gecko to cling to slippery surfaces, even vertical ones.

FACT FILE
Name Flying gecko
(Ptychozoon kuhli)
Size 4 in (9.5 cm) long
Distribution Indonesia and
Malaysian Peninsula

TIGER CENTIPEDES

LARGE, POISONOUS CENTIPEDES scurry across the rain forest floor searching for prey. They feed mainly on insects and spiders, but also catch small toads, snakes, and mammals. Their poison fangs are formidable weapons. Giant tiger centipedes like this one can easily dry out, so they emerge only at night, when the forest is cool and damp. During the day, the tiger centipede hides under leaves, logs, and bark where the air is moist. The female digs a hole in the earth under a stone and lays her eggs there. She curls her long body around the eggs to protect them. When they hatch, the young centipedes have just as many legs as their parents. They have to molt in order to grow, because their hard outer skin, called the exoskeleton, will not stretch as they grow bigger.

Two long, jointed antennae help the centipede feel its way around and detect food.

These mouthparts tear up food.

On the end of the poison fang, there is a curved tip that injects poison into a victim.

FEARSOME FANGS
Centipedes stun their prey with the large poison claws just below the head. They hold the victim firmly in their fangs and then tear it to pieces with their mouthparts. The centipede eats only the soft parts of its prey.

Close up, you can see tiny creatures called mites that live on the centipede.

There are four simple eyes on each side of the head.

Each poison fang has four sections.

LOADS OF LEGS

With its many long legs and flattened body, the centipede can run quickly and smoothly over, under, and around the plants of the rain forest. The legs lift the body off the ground so that it does not catch against leaves or twigs. Tiger centipedes can have as many as 23 pairs of legs.

FACT FILE
Name Tiger centipede (*Scolopendra gigantea*)
Size 9.5 in (24 cm) long
Distribution Central and South America

TOXIC TIGER

Vivid orange and black tiger stripes warn enemies that this centipede is poisonous. Predators soon learn to leave it alone.

Claws on the ends of the legs grip onto trees and rocks.

The legs are attached to the sides of the body.

These jointed legs bend easily.

A hard exoskeleton protects the soft inner body.

Two large legs at the end of the abdomen hold the centipede's prey still while it injects poison into it.

Each segment of the body has one breathing hole, called a spiracle.

The bright colors warn other animals that the centipede is poisonous.

FURRY FLIERS

SHY, SECRETIVE fruit bats leave the trees at dusk and fly over the forest canopy to search for food. They cannot turn well as they fly, and prefer to avoid the thick plant growth lower down in the forest. Fruit bats feed mainly on fruits like figs, mangoes, and bananas. They spit out seeds from these fruits, or pass them out in their droppings, and this helps the trees to spread throughout the forest. Many bats live in large groups, but male Franquet's fruit bats usually roost (rest) alone. The females sometimes roost in groups when they are nursing their young. Bats are blind and hairless when they are born. They cling onto their mother's fur, and drink her milk. After a few weeks, the young bats have fur too, and they start learning how to fly.

FACT FILE
Name Franquet's fruit bat
(Epomops franqueti)
Size Wingspan 14 in (36 cm)
Distribution Central and Western Africa

JUICE EXTRACTOR

Franquet's fruit bat sucks out the juices from tropical fruits. It puts its lips around the fruit and bites into the flesh with its teeth. Then the bat squashes the fruit with its strong tongue and sucks out the juices.

The bat flexes these arm bones up and down to flap its wings.

The skin is tightly stretched between the bones so that the wings are both light and strong.

SKINNY WINGS

Bats are the only mammals that can really fly. Their wings are made of an elastic membrane covered with skin. This is stretched between the four very long fingers on each hand. Bats lick their wings to keep them clean and in good condition for flying. On a hot day, they flap their wings like fans to keep themselves cool.

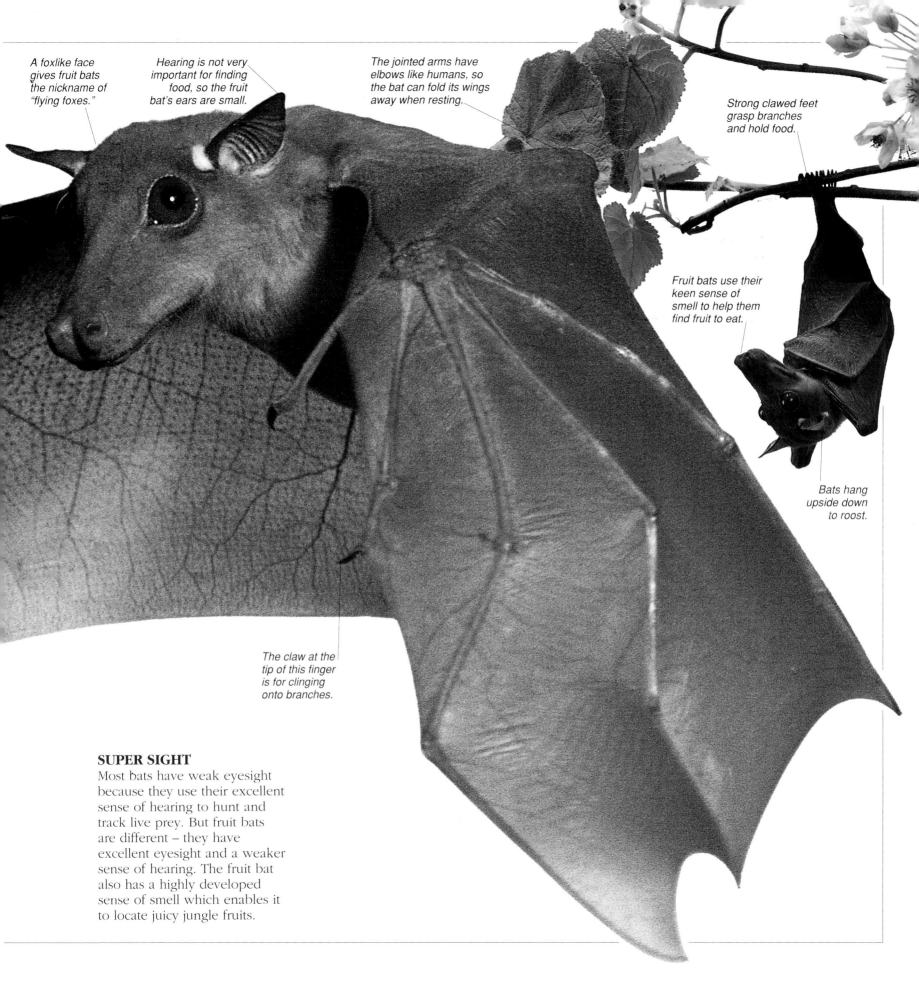

A foxlike face gives fruit bats the nickname of "flying foxes."

Hearing is not very important for finding food, so the fruit bat's ears are small.

The jointed arms have elbows like humans, so the bat can fold its wings away when resting.

Strong clawed feet grasp branches and hold food.

Fruit bats use their keen sense of smell to help them find fruit to eat.

Bats hang upside down to roost.

The claw at the tip of this finger is for clinging onto branches.

SUPER SIGHT

Most bats have weak eyesight because they use their excellent sense of hearing to hunt and track live prey. But fruit bats are different – they have excellent eyesight and a weaker sense of hearing. The fruit bat also has a highly developed sense of smell which enables it to locate juicy jungle fruits.

SPIKY SPIDERS

THESE STRANGELY SHAPED spiders look almost unreal as they scuttle around on their huge, fragile webs. Spiny-bellied orb weavers, such as these, make their homes among the leaves and flowers of mangrove trees. The spiky shape and the bright, shiny patterns on their bodies make them easy to spot. But the spikes also make the spiders difficult to eat, and this puts off birds, lizards, and other predators looking for a meal. These female spiders are fat with eggs. When they lay their eggs, they wrap them in a bright green cocoon made of silk. They attach the cocoon to the underside of a mangrove leaf, where it is well hidden. The young hatch inside the cocoon, molt their skin once, and bite their way through to the outside world.

FACT FILE
Name Spiny-bellied orb weaver
(Gasteracantha cancriformis)
Size Body 0.5 in (1.5 cm) wide
Distribution The Americas

The spider's abdomen is smooth and shiny. Rainwater runs off it quickly, so it does not become waterlogged.

These cone-shaped spikes are made of a hard protein called chitin.

Each thread is thin and stretchy, but it is also very strong.

Some of these tiny hairs on the spider's legs are very sensitive to touch. Others can detect the air currents made by flying insects.

This tough cuticle (outer skin) protects the spider's body.

FOOD STORAGE
Spiders are fierce predators, with mouthparts adapted to dealing quickly with struggling prey. Some of the insects that blunder into a web have stingers, or other weapons, which they could use to attack the spider if they had the chance. So the spiky spider bites her prey with her sharp fangs. These inject a venom that paralyzes the insect without killing it, so the flesh stays fresh until the spider needs to eat it.

Three minute claws on each foot help the spider grip its web and move quickly toward a trapped insect.

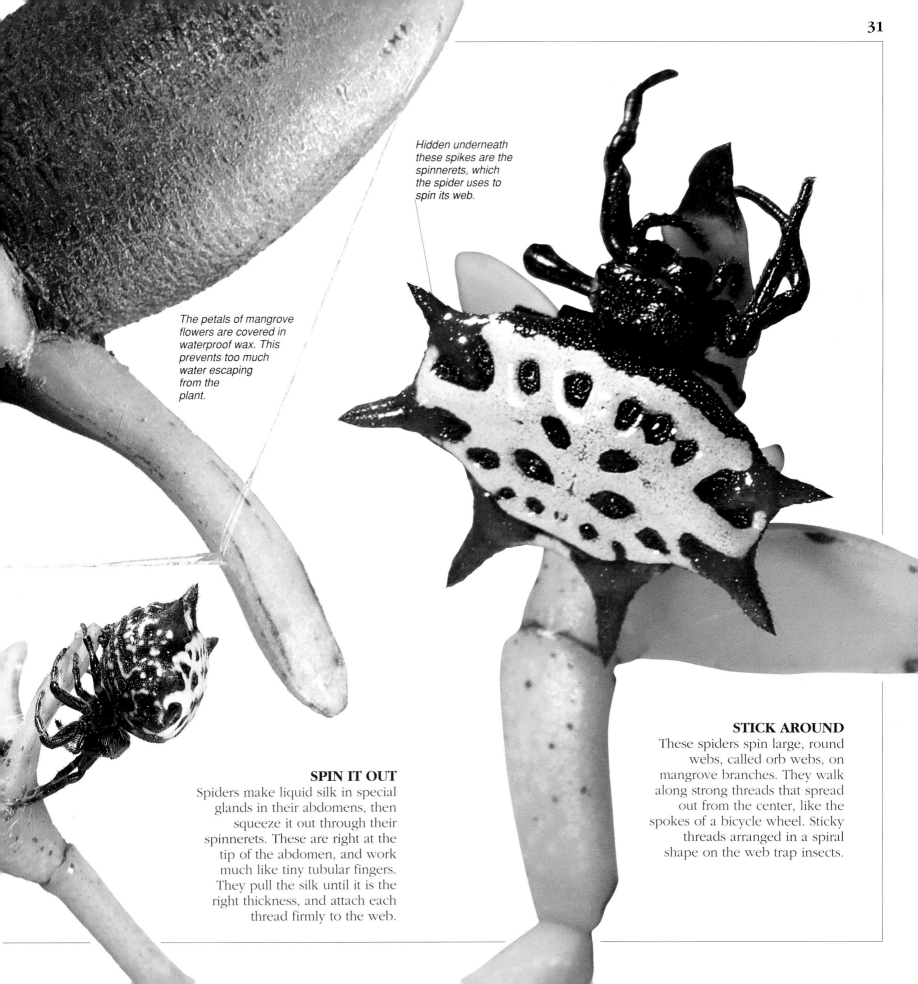

Hidden underneath these spikes are the spinnerets, which the spider uses to spin its web.

The petals of mangrove flowers are covered in waterproof wax. This prevents too much water escaping from the plant.

SPIN IT OUT

Spiders make liquid silk in special glands in their abdomens, then squeeze it out through their spinnerets. These are right at the tip of the abdomen, and work much like tiny tubular fingers. They pull the silk until it is the right thickness, and attach each thread firmly to the web.

STICK AROUND

These spiders spin large, round webs, called orb webs, on mangrove branches. They walk along strong threads that spread out from the center, like the spokes of a bicycle wheel. Sticky threads arranged in a spiral shape on the web trap insects.

STICKY-FINGERED FROGS

THE DAMP, SHADY RAIN FOREST makes an ideal home for frogs. They need to live in moist places because their skin is not waterproof and dries out quickly. Frogs also need pools of water for their tadpoles to live in while they grow into adults. Some rain forest frogs lay their eggs on a leaf or a patch of ground that they have carefully cleared. When the tadpoles of poison dart frogs hatch, they wriggle onto one of their parent's backs. The adult frog carries the tadpoles to a pool of water in the center of the leaves of plants called bromeliads. Tree frogs and poison dart frogs have large, sticky suckers on their fingers and toes. The suckers help them cling onto smooth, wet leaves and mossy branches. In fact, tree frogs can cling upside down in the forest for many hours.

FLABBY FROG

White's tree frogs are often very fat, with folds of flesh on their bodies. The skin on their bellies is loose and helps the frogs grip as they climb up slippery tree trunks. Many tree frogs are green or brown to help them blend in with the colors of the forest and hide from enemies. Tree frogs usually hide by day and come out only at night.

Two large eyes allow the frog to see well in daylight and also at night when it hunts for food.

The wide mouth houses a sticky tongue for catching beetles, moths, and other insects.

The skin on the frog's throat expands like a balloon to make a loud mating call.

These long, thin toes curl around leaves and twigs for a strong hold.

Whenever the frog blinks, its eyelids slide across the eyes to wipe them clean.

There is an eardrum on each side of the head. The frog can hear a wide range of sounds.

FACT FILE
Name White's tree frog
  (Litoria caerulea)
Size 2.5 in (6 cm) long
Distribution Australia

A poison dart frog's brilliant warning colors may be yellow, red, green, or blue.

DON'T EAT ME
The poison dart frog's brilliant colors warn enemies that it is dangerous. These frogs have special glands in their skin that produce a deadly poison. The poison can paralyze a bird or monkey immediately, so those animals soon learn to leave the frogs alone. The most deadly kind of dart frog contains enough poison to kill six people.

STICKY FEET
Each finger and toe has a pad on the underside. These pads produce a sticky substance called mucus. The sticky mucus helps the frog grip wet leaves and other slimy surfaces. With their sticky feet, tree frogs can even climb up slippery tree trunks.

Sticky pads on each finger are for climbing.

FOREST ORCHIDS

THESE TROPICAL ORCHIDS perch high on the branches of the tallest trees, where they are close to the sunlight. These orchids are epiphytes and have long, trailing roots to soak up moisture from the air. They also store food and water in swollen stems called pseudobulbs. Their colorful, scented flowers attract insects. The insects eat the nectar made by the flower, then carry its pollen to other orchids. If a flower receives pollen from another of the same kind, seeds may develop. Orchids produce thousands of tiny, light seeds that drift through the forest on the wind. If they land in a suitable spot, they will grow into new orchid plants.

Clusters of pollen are near the top of the flower.

The labellum of this flower forms a flat landing platform for insects.

POLLEN PARCELS
Most flowers have loose, dust-like pollen. But orchids have special clusters called pollinia consisting of thousands of pollen grains. Each cluster has a special pad at its base. The pad sticks to the head of a visiting insect, which then carries it to another orchid flower.

Below the pollinia is the stigma (the tip of the female part).

FANTASTIC FLOWER
These orchids are unusual flowers. The stem of the male part (the stamen) and the stem of the female part (the style) are joined together in a central column. One of the orchid's petals, called the labellum, is a special shape to attract the right kind of insect. The insect cannot get to the nectar it feeds on without becoming covered in pollen.

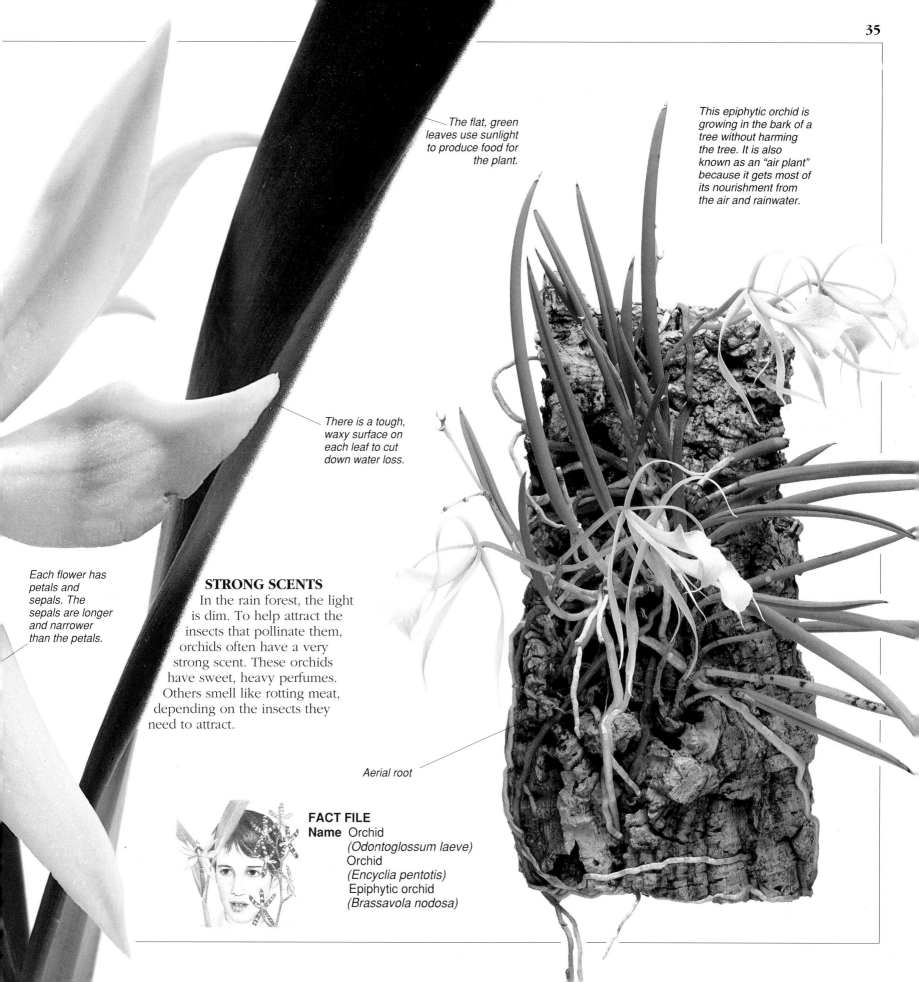

The flat, green leaves use sunlight to produce food for the plant.

This epiphytic orchid is growing in the bark of a tree without harming the tree. It is also known as an "air plant" because it gets most of its nourishment from the air and rainwater.

There is a tough, waxy surface on each leaf to cut down water loss.

Each flower has petals and sepals. The sepals are longer and narrower than the petals.

STRONG SCENTS

In the rain forest, the light is dim. To help attract the insects that pollinate them, orchids often have a very strong scent. These orchids have sweet, heavy perfumes. Others smell like rotting meat, depending on the insects they need to attract.

Aerial root

FACT FILE
Name Orchid
(Odontoglossum laeve)
Orchid
(Encyclia pentotis)
Epiphytic orchid
(Brassavola nodosa)

LEAPING LIZARDS

GREEN IGUANAS ENJOY sunbathing in the leafy branches of mangrove trees. Their bright color helps conceal them from predators. If they are alarmed, these sprightly lizards jump into the mangrove swamp and swim to safety. Male iguanas protect their territory by scaring away other males with a fierce display. They stand up tall, flatten their bodies, and stick out their dewlaps (neck flaps). This usually puts off the intruder, and real fights do not often take place. After mating, each female digs a burrow in warm, damp soil, and lays 20 to 30 eggs there. When the young hatch, they sleep and feed together, relying on safety in numbers, until they are old enough to protect themselves.

FACT FILE
Name Green iguana
(Iguana iguana)
Size Body 6 in (15 cm) long
Distribution Central and South America and The Caribbean

SPEEDY SPRINTER
With its long legs and clawed toes, this iguana is a fast mover. Its body is streamlined for speed, and the long tail helps it balance as it jumps. It sprints very fast, can run up tree trunks, and leap from branch to branch. Iguanas are mainly herbivorous (plant-eating), so they do not have to hunt for prey, but they do need to escape from hungry enemies, such as birds.

The iguana uses its tail to balance the weight of its body. This is called counterbalancing.

The powerful back legs are good for running and jumping.

Scaly skin protects the body from damage, and stops it from drying out.

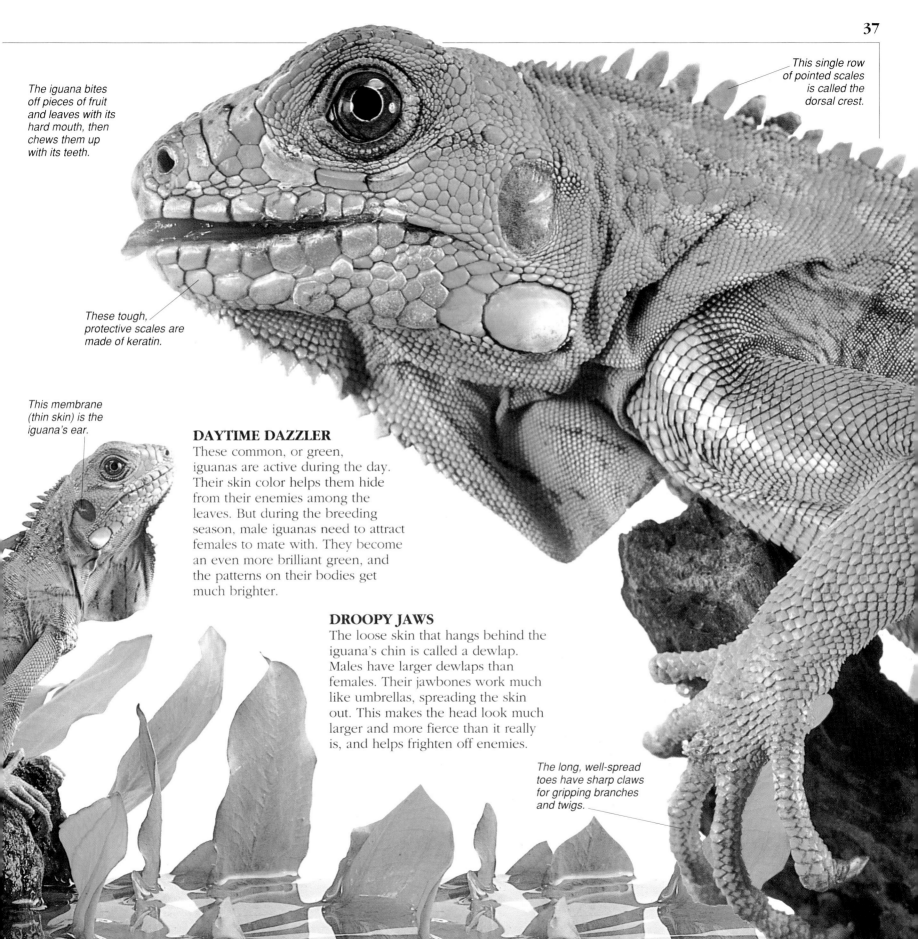

This single row of pointed scales is called the dorsal crest.

The iguana bites off pieces of fruit and leaves with its hard mouth, then chews them up with its teeth.

These tough, protective scales are made of keratin.

This membrane (thin skin) is the iguana's ear.

DAYTIME DAZZLER

These common, or green, iguanas are active during the day. Their skin color helps them hide from their enemies among the leaves. But during the breeding season, male iguanas need to attract females to mate with. They become an even more brilliant green, and the patterns on their bodies get much brighter.

DROOPY JAWS

The loose skin that hangs behind the iguana's chin is called a dewlap. Males have larger dewlaps than females. Their jawbones work much like umbrellas, spreading the skin out. This makes the head look much larger and more fierce than it really is, and helps frighten off enemies.

The long, well-spread toes have sharp claws for gripping branches and twigs.

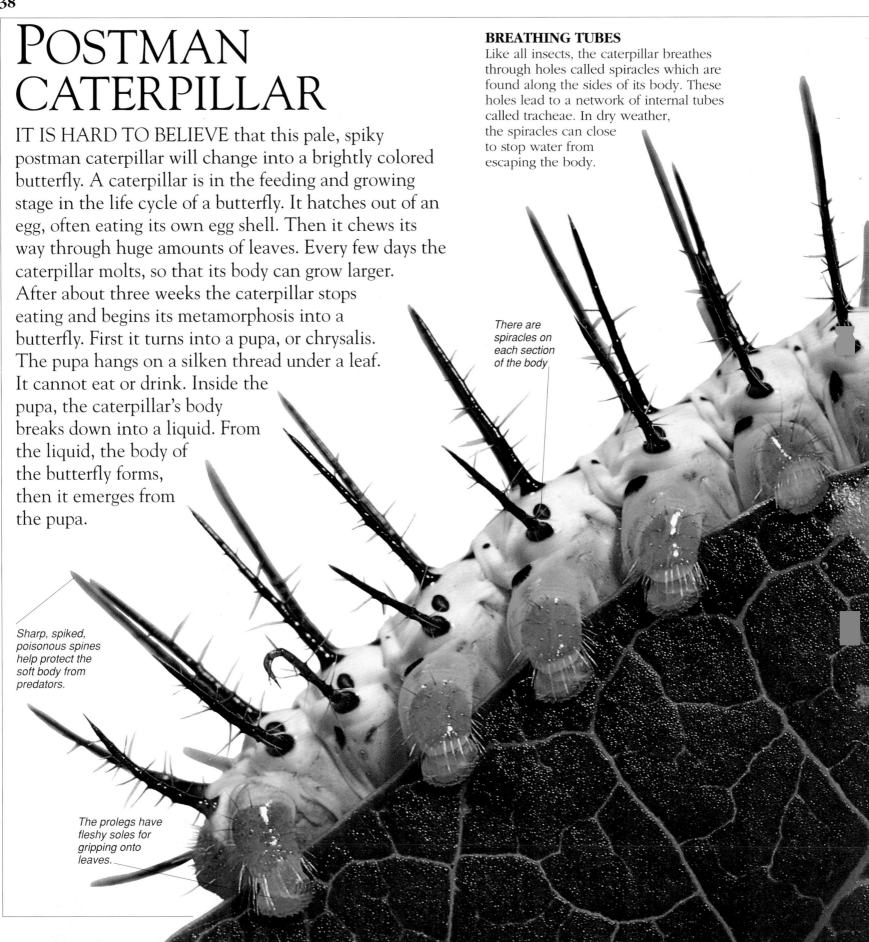

POSTMAN CATERPILLAR

IT IS HARD TO BELIEVE that this pale, spiky postman caterpillar will change into a brightly colored butterfly. A caterpillar is in the feeding and growing stage in the life cycle of a butterfly. It hatches out of an egg, often eating its own egg shell. Then it chews its way through huge amounts of leaves. Every few days the caterpillar molts, so that its body can grow larger. After about three weeks the caterpillar stops eating and begins its metamorphosis into a butterfly. First it turns into a pupa, or chrysalis. The pupa hangs on a silken thread under a leaf. It cannot eat or drink. Inside the pupa, the caterpillar's body breaks down into a liquid. From the liquid, the body of the butterfly forms, then it emerges from the pupa.

BREATHING TUBES

Like all insects, the caterpillar breathes through holes called spiracles which are found along the sides of its body. These holes lead to a network of internal tubes called tracheae. In dry weather, the spiracles can close to stop water from escaping the body.

There are spiracles on each section of the body

Sharp, spiked, poisonous spines help protect the soft body from predators.

The prolegs have fleshy soles for gripping onto leaves.

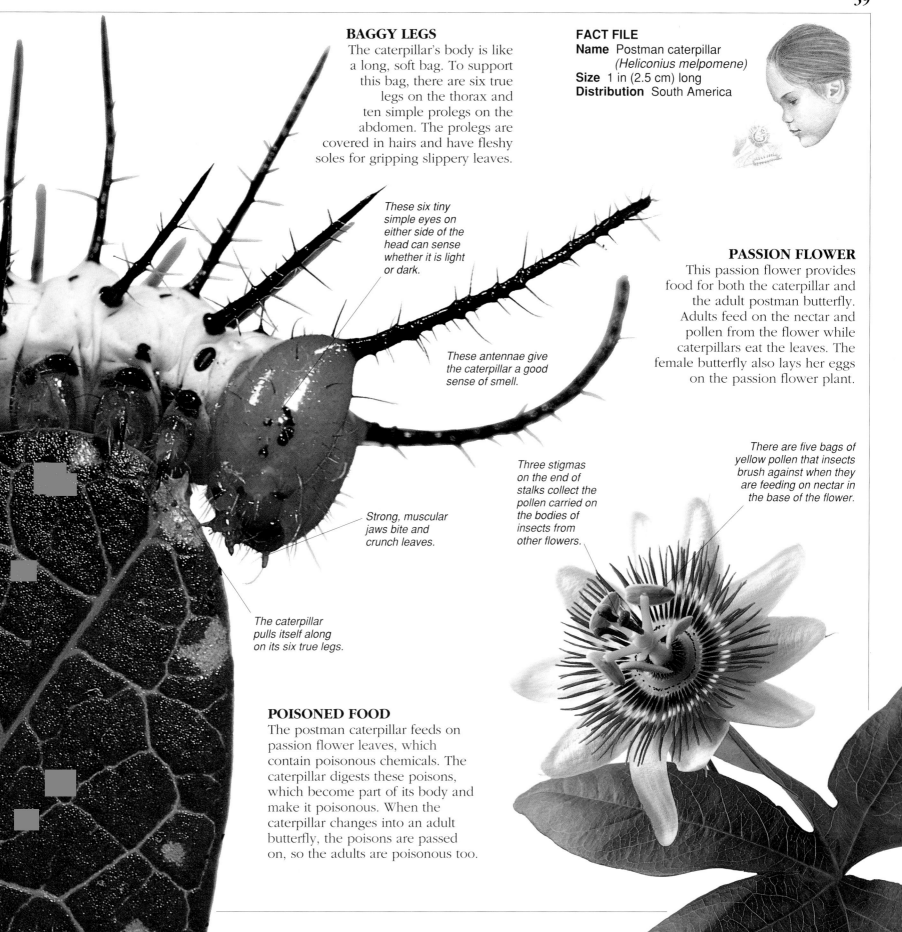

BAGGY LEGS

The caterpillar's body is like a long, soft bag. To support this bag, there are six true legs on the thorax and ten simple prolegs on the abdomen. The prolegs are covered in hairs and have fleshy soles for gripping slippery leaves.

FACT FILE
Name Postman caterpillar
(*Heliconius melpomene*)
Size 1 in (2.5 cm) long
Distribution South America

These six tiny simple eyes on either side of the head can sense whether it is light or dark.

These antennae give the caterpillar a good sense of smell.

PASSION FLOWER

This passion flower provides food for both the caterpillar and the adult postman butterfly. Adults feed on the nectar and pollen from the flower while caterpillars eat the leaves. The female butterfly also lays her eggs on the passion flower plant.

Strong, muscular jaws bite and crunch leaves.

Three stigmas on the end of stalks collect the pollen carried on the bodies of insects from other flowers.

There are five bags of yellow pollen that insects brush against when they are feeding on nectar in the base of the flower.

The caterpillar pulls itself along on its six true legs.

POISONED FOOD

The postman caterpillar feeds on passion flower leaves, which contain poisonous chemicals. The caterpillar digests these poisons, which become part of its body and make it poisonous. When the caterpillar changes into an adult butterfly, the poisons are passed on, so the adults are poisonous too.

POSTMAN BUTTERFLY

WHEN THIS POSTMAN butterfly pulls itself out of its pupa, its wings are soft, damp, and crushed. It takes about an hour for them to stretch and dry out. The main purpose in the life of adult butterflies is to find a mate and lay eggs. The male postman butterfly takes three months to mature before he can mate. The female lays 400 to 500 eggs because so many of the young caterpillars will be eaten by insects and spiders. She lays about 20 eggs at a time on the tender leaves and shoots of passion flower vines. She avoids plants with other eggs or caterpillars on them because caterpillars often eat each other.

Close up, you can see the scales that give the wings their color.

FACT FILE
Name Postman butterfly
(*Heliconius melpomene*)
Size Wingspan 1.25 in (3 cm)
Distribution South America

SCALY WINGS

Each wing is covered with thousands of tiny, overlapping scales that give the wings their color. Butterflies and moths belong to a group of insects called *Lepidoptera*, which means "scaled wing."

When it is not being used, the proboscis is curled up under the head, out of the way.

Six jointed legs are joined to the middle part of the body, called the thorax.

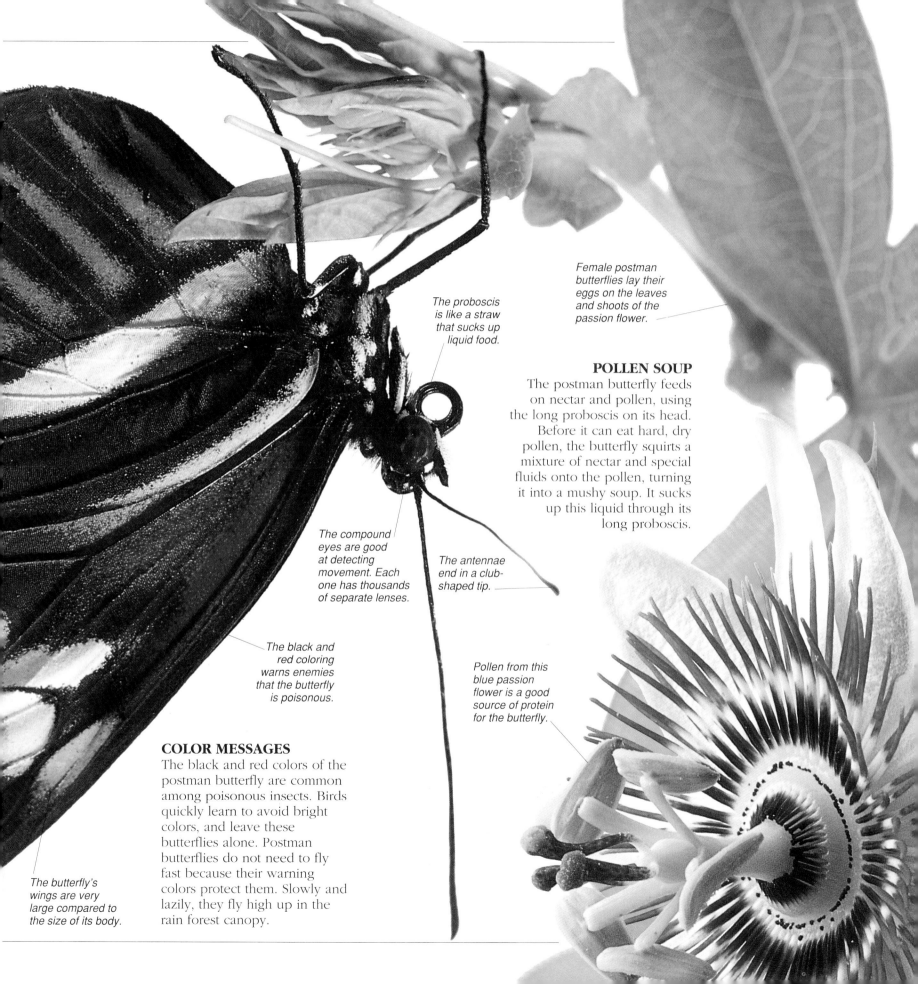

The proboscis is like a straw that sucks up liquid food.

Female postman butterflies lay their eggs on the leaves and shoots of the passion flower.

POLLEN SOUP

The postman butterfly feeds on nectar and pollen, using the long proboscis on its head. Before it can eat hard, dry pollen, the butterfly squirts a mixture of nectar and special fluids onto the pollen, turning it into a mushy soup. It sucks up this liquid through its long proboscis.

The compound eyes are good at detecting movement. Each one has thousands of separate lenses.

The antennae end in a club-shaped tip.

The black and red coloring warns enemies that the butterfly is poisonous.

Pollen from this blue passion flower is a good source of protein for the butterfly.

COLOR MESSAGES

The black and red colors of the postman butterfly are common among poisonous insects. Birds quickly learn to avoid bright colors, and leave these butterflies alone. Postman butterflies do not need to fly fast because their warning colors protect them. Slowly and lazily, they fly high up in the rain forest canopy.

The butterfly's wings are very large compared to the size of its body.

PLANT PARADISE

THE WARM environment of a mangrove swamp is perfect for plant life. Many different kinds of plants flourish here, including mosses, ferns, and trees. Some are completely aquatic, which means that they live submerged in the water. Water lettuces and water hyacinths float on the surface with their roots in the water. These plants can be carried along by water currents and breezes. The waterproof leaves have air-filled floats to keep them the right side up. Other plants, such as mangrove trees, grow in the shallow water at the edge of the swamp. Their roots are firmly embedded in wet sand or mud. All swamp animals, including birds, insects, fish, and mammals, depend on the plants for food, and also for the oxygen that they produce. If there were no plants, the animals would all disappear, too.

SALT SOLUTION

Mangroves are the only trees that grow in salt water. Each kind has special roots that are adapted to help it breathe. These red mangroves have prop roots, which are partly exposed to the air. Oxygen enters through tiny holes, called lenticels, in the bark of the roots. Too much salt is poisonous to plants, and makes it difficult for them to take up water. The mangrove's leaves are waterproof, which keeps water from escaping.

SWAMP SALAD

When the water lettuce plant has space around it, it is a neat rosette of leaves floating on the water. New rosettes sprout at the tips of short stems, called stolons, that grow out at the sides. These eventually break off to form new plants. Water lettuces can quickly cover the surface. As they become more crowded, the leaves have less room to spread out, so they grow straight up.

There are silky hairs covering the leaves. Water rolls off them, so they do not become waterlogged and sink below the surface.

A spongy, air-filled swelling at the base of each leaf stalk keeps the plant afloat.

The leaves are broad and flat, to absorb as much sunlight as possible. Through a process called photosynthesis, the plant converts sunlight into its food.

This water lettuce plant has plenty of room to spread its leaves out over the water's surface.

These trailing, feathery roots absorb nutrients from the water.

FACT FILE
Name Water hyacinth
(*Eichhornia crassipes*)
Size Leaves 6 in (15 cm) long
Flower spike 5 in (12 cm) long
Distribution Worldwide

POLLUTION PATROL
The roots of water hyacinths and water lettuces are very good at absorbing important nutrients from the water. They also trap substances that pollute the water. Scientists have begun to use these floating plants to filter (strain) the water in polluted rivers and lakes.

The scent of water hyacinth flowers attracts insects, such as butterflies, that pollinate the plant.

Mangrove leaves are waterproof, to prevent too much water from evaporating into the air.

Like mangrove leaves, water hyacinth leaves have a waxy cuticle (skin) so they do not become waterlogged.

CAIMAN CRUNCH

FLOATING IN THE STILL water of a tropical swamp or lake, these caimans often look like harmless logs. They are related to alligators, and like them, their eyes and nostrils are set high up on the head. This means that even when the rest of the caiman's body is under water, it can see and breathe in air. Although this young caiman is small, it is a fierce predator, feeding mainly on insects and frogs. Adults prey on larger animals, including fish and mammals. In the breeding season, female caimans gather bits of plants with their mouths, then build huge mounds for their eggs. Each female lays up to 40 eggs in the middle of her mound. The rotting vegetation helps keep the eggs warm. After about three months, tiny caimans hatch out. They stay together in groups, watched over by one of the females, until they are strong enough to protect themselves from enemies, such as large snakes.

NO ESCAPE

When a caiman opens its mouth, you can see daggerlike teeth on both jaws. These jaws can snap shut on their prey with great force. The front teeth interlock, so there is little chance of escape for the unfortunate victim. Caimans cannot chew. If their prey is too big to swallow whole, they have to tear off bite-sized chunks.

Strong, sharp teeth crunch through shells.

The caiman's slit-shaped pupils help it hunt at night. The pupils expand in the dark, to make the best use of whatever light there is.

The caiman's snout turns up at the end, keeping the nostrils out of the water.

This dull, blotchy coloring helps a young caiman hide from hungry predators until it is large enough to defend itself.

A flattened, muscular tail like this is ideal for swimming.

The front feet are good for digging. In dry weather, caimans often burrow into the mud, to shelter from the sun.

A caiman's legs are attached to the sides of its body. Caimans can run quite fast, but only over short distances.

BLACK WITH COLD

When caimans get too cold, they change their color. There are cells in the skin that contain a black pigment, called melanin. These cells expand when the temperature drops, and the skin turns black. Dark colors absorb heat well, so a black skin helps the caiman keep warm.

This bony ridge looks much like a pair of glasses, so this caiman is called a spectacled caiman.

Caimans have very good hearing, both in and out of water. Their ears are covered with a thin membrane to keep water from getting inside.

Unlike most reptiles, a caiman does not shed its skin in one piece in order to grow. Instead, it sheds each scale separately, replacing it with a larger one.

This young caiman is only 18 in. long. But it may grow to be up to 8 ft. from head to tail.

FACT FILE
Name Spectacled caiman (young)
(Caiman crocodilus)
Size 18 in (45 cm) long
Distribution Central and South America and Florida

SKIN AND BONES

Like all reptiles, caimans are covered in scales. Their scales are tough, to protect the body from damage. They also prevent the caiman from drying out when it is basking in the sun. Along the back and belly the protective layer is even tougher, because underneath the outer scales there are plates of bone. These are called osteoderms, which means "skin-bones."

TEMPERATE FORESTS

A TEMPERATE FOREST consists of deciduous broad-leaved trees, sometimes with coniferous trees. These forests grow in parts of the world where there is a temperate climate, with distinct winter and summer seasons. Flowering plants on the forest floor have adapted to these changing seasons. They flower and produce their seed in early spring, before the trees produce new leaves and form a thick canopy that blocks out the sun.

NEEDLES
Evergreen coniferous trees have needles instead of leaves. The needles have a waxy coating that protects them from freezing during the cold winter months.

Pine needles and cones

A CHANGE OF COLOR
Each autumn, deciduous trees change color to orange and brown. In winter they lose their foliage and the forest floor is carpeted with a layer of dead leaves. This layer is called leaf litter.

Blackberry

NUTS AND FRUITS
Fruits such as acorns, beech nuts, hawthorn berries, and blackberries provide forest mammals and birds with an important source of food during the winter.

Acorn and oak leaves

THE LIFE OF A TREE
A broad-leaved tree such as an oak supports all kinds of animal life and is an ecosystem in itself. An oak tree produces its own food, and its leaves, fruits, flowers, bark, and wood are eaten by the insects, birds, and small mammals that live in and around the tree.

Gall wasps lay eggs on the buds of oak trees, which form galls.

Woodpeckers nest in holes in the tree trunk.

Several kinds of fungi grow around the base of the tree and on the bark.

Squirrels bury acorns from the tree to eat in winter.

Wood lice and beetles live in the leaf litter and under loose bark.

Centipedes hunt small creatures living on and around the tree.

INSECTS

Many insect eggs hatch in the spring so that the larvae can feed on new leaves. Beetles, ants, and other crawling insects eat dead animal and plant material in the leaf litter.

Stag beetle

BIRDS

Some birds in temperate forests migrate to warmer places in winter and return each spring to nest and rear their young. But an owl may spend its whole life in the same forest, hunting at night for small mammals such as mice and shrews.

Great horned owl

MAMMALS

Many small mammals hibernate in winter. Their temperature drops, and their body fat keeps them alive. Some mammals, such as chipmunks wake up every now and then to eat their store of nuts.

Chipmunk

Common salamander

REPTILES AND AMPHIBIANS

Many forest reptiles and amphibians, such as salamanders and toads, hide under a log or rock during the day and come out at dusk to find food.

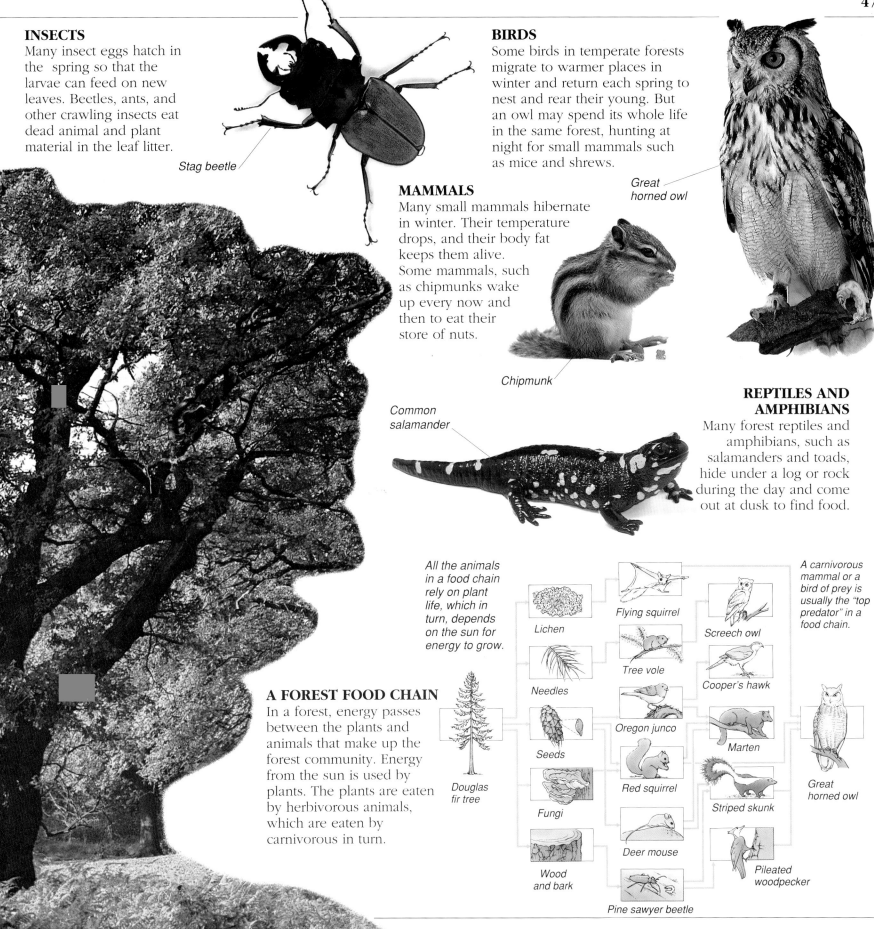

All the animals in a food chain rely on plant life, which in turn, depends on the sun for energy to grow.

A carnivorous mammal or a bird of prey is usually the "top predator" in a food chain.

A FOREST FOOD CHAIN

In a forest, energy passes between the plants and animals that make up the forest community. Energy from the sun is used by plants. The plants are eaten by herbivorous animals, which are eaten by carnivorous in turn.

Lichen

Needles

Seeds

Fungi

Wood and bark

Douglas fir tree

Flying squirrel

Tree vole

Oregon junco

Red squirrel

Deer mouse

Pine sawyer beetle

Screech owl

Cooper's hawk

Marten

Striped skunk

Pileated woodpecker

Great horned owl

SPEEDY SQUIRREL

THE GRAY SQUIRREL travels nimbly through the branches of temperate trees in search of food. If danger threatens, it may stay completely still, relying on its mottled gray color to hide it against tree trunks. But if it is spotted by an enemy, such as a bird of prey, the squirrel's speedy acrobatics make it difficult to catch. The gray squirrel builds a round, football-sized nest, called a drey, in the fork of a tree. The drey is made of twigs, and lined with soft materials, such as grass and leaves. In spring, and often in summer, too, the female gives birth to two or three young. At first, they have no fur and cannot see. After two or three months, the young squirrels leave the drey and begin to fend for themselves.

The top layer of fur is made up of long, stiff hairs. Close up, you can see that these outer hairs are colored brown, black, and white.

Long, strong claws grip tightly onto smooth, slippery branches.

NUT NIBBLER
Trees provide squirrels with food all year-round. In fall and winter, they feed mainly on fruit and seeds, such as acorns, beechnuts, and pinecones. In spring and summer, squirrels eat catkins and buds, and strip the bark from trees in order to feed on the juicy sap underneath. Gray squirrels also eat fungi, insects, and young birds.

Squirrels sit up to feed, holding food in their front paws.

SQUIRREL SIGNALS
Gray squirrels use sounds, scents, and body language, such as flapping the tail, to communicate with each other. These signals tell other squirrels about food, warn them of danger, or attract a mate.

If the squirrel spots an enemy, it may warn others by displaying this patch of white fur.

These long back feet help the animal balance.

FACT FILE
Name Gray squirrel (young)
(*Sciurus carolinensis*)
Size Body 3 in (8 cm) long
Distribution Europe, North
America, and Southern Africa

TIGHTROPE TRICKS

Squirrels leap gracefully from branch to branch, using their tails like rudders to change direction. They can balance on the flimsiest of twigs, and easily run up and down smooth tree trunks by clinging on with their sharp claws. On the ground, squirrels often stop and sit upright to sniff the air for danger.

SURVIVAL SKILLS

In winter, the gray squirrel spends much of its time sheltering in its drey. Before the cold weather arrives, the squirrel eats as much food as it can to build up stores of fat in its body. This will help it survive when food is hard to find. It also buries nuts in the ground, and uses its excellent sense of smell to find them again.

Grayish brown fur helps hide the squirrel among bark and leaves.

Long, sensitive whiskers help the squirrel feel its way around.

These young squirrels are just a few months old.

Squirrels can fluff up their tails to make themselves look larger and more fearsome.

PARENT BUGS

THROUGHOUT THE SUMMER, parent bugs are found on the leaves of birch trees, feeding on the juicy sap. Most other insects lay their eggs, then leave them to fend for themselves. But the female parent bug is a good mother, caring for her young and protecting them from enemies such as birds. That is why this kind of bug is called a parent bug. The female lays between 30 and 40 tiny eggs on the underside of a birch leaf. Then she stands guard over them, hiding them underneath her body, until they hatch two to three weeks later. Unlike many insects, which hatch as larvae (grubs), bugs hatch as nymphs, miniature versions of the adults, but without wings. The young parent bugs remain close together under their mother's body. Eventually, as the nymphs grow, they wander off to live by themselves. They molt several times before they are full-grown adults with wings.

WINTER HIDEAWAY

Unlike many insects, parent bugs survive through the winter. They hide under flakes of bark and in wood cracks to avoid predators such as birds. When new birch leaves begin to open in the spring, the bugs come out again and start to feed.

MINIATURE SHIELDS

A bug's exoskeleton is rigid, so it has to molt in order to grow. It sheds its skin several times before it is fully grown. After its final molt, the bug has wings. Parent bugs look just like shields when they fold their wings. That is why they are often called shield bugs.

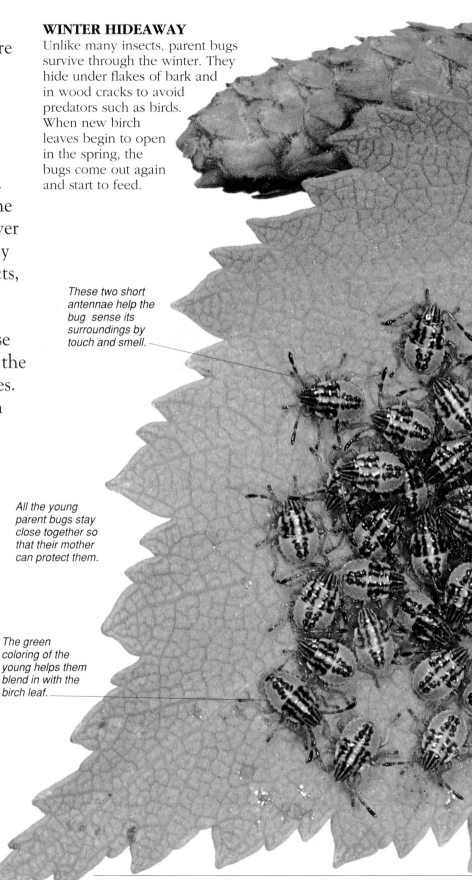

These two short antennae help the bug sense its surroundings by touch and smell.

All the young parent bugs stay close together so that their mother can protect them.

The green coloring of the young helps them blend in with the birch leaf.

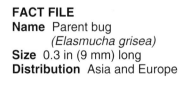

FACT FILE
Name Parent bug
  (Elasmucha grisea)
Size 0.3 in (9 mm) long
Distribution Asia and Europe

From above, it is easy to see why these bugs are also known as shield bugs.

This area of the forewing is hard. It protects the body underneath.

The compound eyes are made up of lots of individual lenses.

The tiny, brightly colored nymph looks similar to the adult, except that it has no wings.

BEAKY BUG

The parent bug has long, narrow mouthparts, with four sharp cutters on the end. It uses these to pierce holes in leaves. Then it sucks up the sap using a tubelike mouthpart, called a rostrum, which is protected inside its beak.

Three pairs of short, jointed legs are attached to the middle part of the body, called the thorax.

The tip of the forewing is a clear membrane.

SALAMANDER SPOTS

ON COOL, WET NIGHTS, the spotted salamander comes out of its forest burrow to hunt for a meal. It makes no sound, unlike its noisy relatives, the frogs and toads. In spring, spotted salamanders travel to a nearby pond, often in large groups, to mate and lay their eggs. Each female lays about 100 eggs in a jelly-covered mass. One or two months later, the larvae hatch out into the water. They have a head and a long tail, and breathe through gills, like fish. They are carnivorous (meat-eating), and feed on small water insects. Over the next few months they develop legs, and their gills are replaced by lungs inside their bodies for breathing air. Eventually, the young salamanders climb out of the pond to begin life on land.

DANGER SPOTS
The two rows of bright yellow spots on this salamander's body warn enemies, such as birds and snakes, to leave it alone. If it is attacked, a milky poison oozes out of special glands at the back of its head. The poison tastes nasty, so the enemy usually looks somewhere else for a meal.

Fungi such as this mushroom also live in damp, shady places.

Yellow spots warn enemies that this salamander is poisonous.

The eyes can see well in the dark.

DOWN UNDER
Spotted salamanders live on land, but they have to stay in damp places. This is because their skin is not waterproof, and it cannot keep in moisture. If a salamander's skin dries out, it will die. For this reason it spends most of its time buried beneath the soil, or under a log or a rock.

The streamlined shape of the salamander's body and tail help it burrow under logs and rocks, and through soil.

The feet end in long, splayed toes for shoveling the soil aside.

The salamander's smooth, moist skin helps it slither through soil easily.

FACT FILE
Name American spotted salamander (*Ambystoma maculatum*)
Size Head and body 6 in (15 cm)
Distribution North America

SLIPPERY SKIN

The salamander's skin is delicate, and sometimes gets damaged as the animal burrows beneath the ground. So every week or two, the outer layer of skin is shed to reveal a new one that has grown underneath. This is called molting.

Adult salamanders have lungs, but they can also breathe through their thin skin.

AFTERNOON SNACK

The spotted salamander usually waits for nightfall before it comes out of its damp hiding place. But sometimes, on rainy days, it lurks in the mouth of its burrow. There it waits to pounce on unsuspecting prey. Small creatures such as insects, worms, slugs, and snails are quickly snapped up in its hungry jaws.

FIRST FLOWERS

IN THE FIRST FEW WEEKS of spring, the forest floor is carpeted with early flowers, such as bluebells and primroses. The leaves fall off the trees in autumn, and provide food for many tiny creatures, such as beetles and other insect larvae. Then flowering plants use the early spring sunshine to bloom and produce seeds before the trees grow new leaves and cover the woodland floor in shade. Bluebells grow from seeds at first, then usually regrow their leaves and flowers each year from the bulbs that form in the soil. Ferns produce simple spores, which do not have their own food supply as seeds do. The plant flicks the spores out, and the wind spreads them. Each spore grows into a tiny, leaflike plant and a new fern grows from this.

The female part, called the stigma, receives pollen from other flowers.

The buds stand up at first, but when the flowers open, they hang downward.

The color around the veins gives this green-veined white butterfly its name.

Each plant has a single flower stalk, with up to 20 flowers. All the flowers grow on one side of the stalk.

On warm days there are plenty of insects around, such as this butterfly, to carry pollen from flower to flower.

Bluebell leaves grow straight up from the bulb.

The narrow leaves push up through the leaf litter in spring.

Bluebells are also called wild hyacinths. The flowers are usually violet-blue, like these, but they can be white or pink also.

SEED BOXES

Bluebells form seeds inside capsules, which are like little boxes with three compartments. When the seeds are ripe they are shiny and black. Then the box splits open so that the seeds can fall to the ground and grow into new plants.

CURLY CROZIERS

Fern leaves grow from a swollen underground stem called a rhizome, which contains stored food. In spring, the young leaves slowly unfurl. They look like little hooks, and they are called croziers, after the crook that a bishop carries during ceremonies. The curled shape helps prevent the soft young leaflets from drying out.

This fern is just beginning to unfurl. The fronds sometimes grow for up to two years before they appear above the ground.

The six petals curl back at the tip, forming a bell shape, so the pollen sacs on the stamens stick out of the flower.

UNDERGROUND PANTRY

Bluebells survive winter as small, white, egg-shaped bulbs buried in the soil. These bulbs contain food that the plant makes and stores during the summer. In spring, the first new leaves use the energy in the stored food to grow.

Sometimes buds grow out of the rhizome and develop into new plants. What looks like a large fern is often several plants growing together.

FACT FILE
Name Bluebell
(*Hyacinthoides non-scripta*)
Distribution Europe

Name Scaly male fern
(*Dryopteris affinis*)
Distribution Europe and Southwest Asia

WAKEFUL WEASELS

BY DAY AND BY NIGHT, these agile weasels run and bound through the forest. They climb well, using their sharp claws to grip smooth or slippery surfaces. Although a weasel is very small, it is a ferocious hunter of other small animals. It is very strong for its size and a male can even kill animals larger than itself, such as young rabbits, when smaller prey is hard to find. In spring, and sometimes in late summer, too, female weasels give birth to a litter of between four and six young, called kittens, in an underground den. The young weasels grow fast and are soon able to join in hunting trips. When they are only three to four months old, they can fend for themselves.

SMALL AND SLENDER
The weasel's long, slender body and short legs help it crawl down small holes, and into cracks in rocks. Females and young weasels, such as this one, can easily follow a mouse or a vole into its burrow and kill it there.

Weasels are very alert and inquisitive. They often stand up on their hind legs to have a good look around.

A weasel's sense of smell is very good.

The weasel's thick, muscular neck allows it to keep a tight hold on a mouse or vole.

A small, slim body like this loses heat quickly. So weasels must eat often in order to keep warm.

These sharp claws grip surfaces and hold on to prey.

FACT FILE
Name Weasel (young)
(*Mustela nivalis*)
Size Body 6 in (15 cm) long
Distribution Asia, Europe,
North Africa, and North America

WINTER WHITE

In cold climates, where it often snows, the weasel molts its brown fur, and grows a white coat for the winter months. This makes it hard for prey and predators to see it against the snowy background. In spring, the weasel grows brown fur on its back once more.

FIERCE HUNTER

Weasels usually hunt alone. But when there are young, the family hunts together, so that the young get some practice before they go off on their own. Adult males catch rats, moles, and toads, as well as insects. Weasels kill small prey by biting it on the back of the neck. But if the prey is large, a weasel attacks the less protected throat.

The ears listen for rustling noises made by prey in the undergrowth.

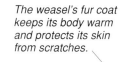
The weasel's fur coat keeps its body warm and protects its skin from scratches.

The weasel's sensitive whiskers help it find its way around, especially in the dark.

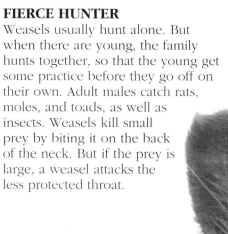

BRIGHT BEETLE

THE BRILLIANTLY colored back of a cardinal beetle makes it easy to recognize. These beetles look like tiny red helicopters as they fly around in spring and early summer, feeding on the pollen of flowers. Female cardinal beetles lay their eggs in cracks in the bark of trees or logs. They choose unhealthy trees, because the eggs hatch into larvae that feed on rotting wood and fungus just beneath the bark. This kind of food is not very nourishing, so it may take a year or more before each larva is ready to pupate (go into a resting stage). The beetles that hatch from each pupa only live for about one month. During this time, they must find and mate with another beetle. To make this easier, cardinal beetles all hatch at about the same time.

The antennae are sensitive to touch. They are also good at detecting smells, even very faint ones.

The wings, the wing cases, and the six legs are all attached to the thorax.

Each wing is made of a thin, transparent skin, called a membrane.

A tough exoskeleton protects the fragile body.

Hooks at the ends of the legs help the beetle climb up trees and cling on to leaves and flowers.

AERODYNAMICS

Cardinal beetles fly through the air quite slowly, using their thin, transparent wings. The wings have no muscles inside. Instead, they are supported by stiff veins, which strengthen them. Special muscles inside the thorax move each wing up and down. When the beetle is not flying, the wings are folded away tightly under the elytra (wing cases).

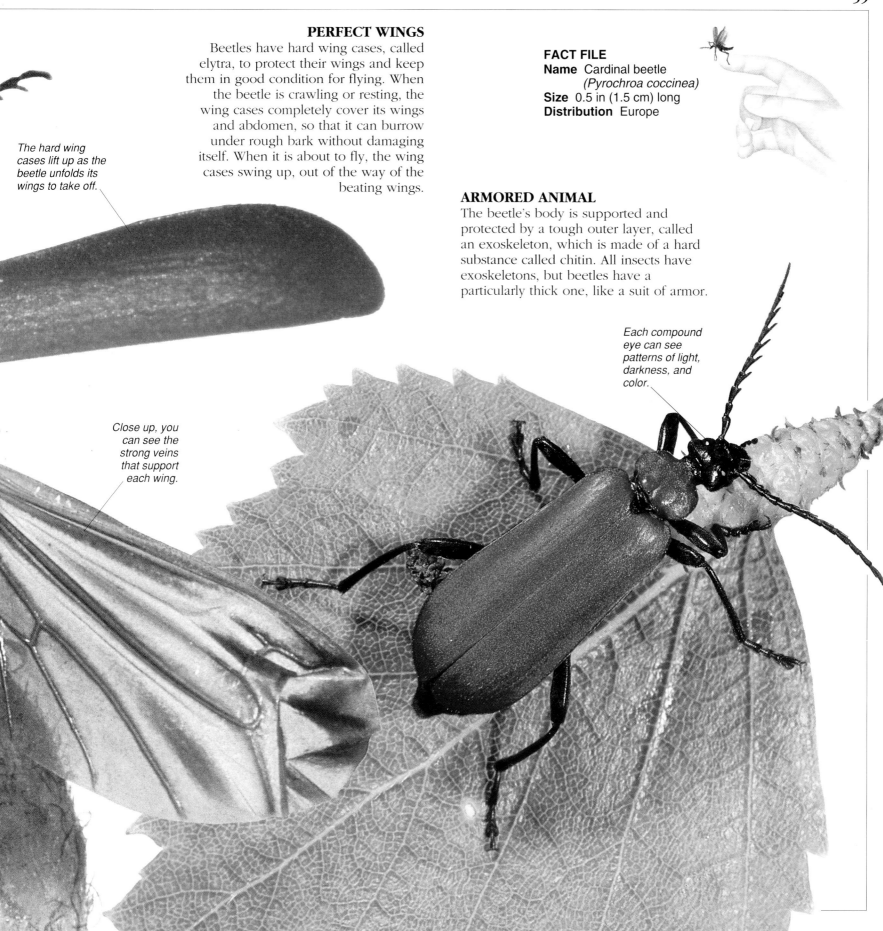

PERFECT WINGS

Beetles have hard wing cases, called elytra, to protect their wings and keep them in good condition for flying. When the beetle is crawling or resting, the wing cases completely cover its wings and abdomen, so that it can burrow under rough bark without damaging itself. When it is about to fly, the wing cases swing up, out of the way of the beating wings.

The hard wing cases lift up as the beetle unfolds its wings to take off.

FACT FILE
Name Cardinal beetle
(Pyrochroa coccinea)
Size 0.5 in (1.5 cm) long
Distribution Europe

ARMORED ANIMAL

The beetle's body is supported and protected by a tough outer layer, called an exoskeleton, which is made of a hard substance called chitin. All insects have exoskeletons, but beetles have a particularly thick one, like a suit of armor.

Each compound eye can see patterns of light, darkness, and color.

Close up, you can see the strong veins that support each wing.

HOOTING OWL

AN UNMISTAKABLE HOOT in the night lets you know that there is a tawny owl in the forest. During the day, the owl sits quietly among the trees. It is hard to spot because its mottled coloring blends in with the bark and leaves. At night, the owl hunts for voles, mice, rats, and small birds. Its sharp hearing and silent flight make it an excellent hunter. Tawny owls nest in hollow trees, or in the old nests of other birds, such as magpies. The female lays between two and four white eggs, and the chicks, called owlets, hatch after about four weeks. The male brings food for the owlets, but sometimes, if prey is hard to find, the biggest owlet eats the smaller ones. The young birds leave the nest after five weeks, but their parents keep feeding them until they are three months old.

FACT FILE
Name Tawny owl
(*Strix aluco*)
Size 1 ft (30 cm) high
Distribution Africa, Asia, and Europe

KEEPING QUIET
Tawny owls can fly very quietly. This enables them to hear the squeaks of their prey, and to pounce without warning. There are fluffy, comblike fringes on the feathers that deaden the sound of the wingbeats. Also, the surfaces of the feathers are velvety. This muffles the sound of the feathers brushing against each other, and the air rushing between them.

The two large ear openings are hidden behind the feathers on these rounded areas of the face.

These huge eyes face forward. They can see very well, even in the dark.

These downy feathers show that this is a young owl.

An owl can turn its head right around until it is facing backward.

Fringes on these flight feathers help the owl fly silently.

SILENT AMBUSH
Owls have such good hearing that they can pick up the squeaks of mice and voles from high above the ground. When the owl hears a possible meal, it glides silently toward its victim. At the last second, it swings its feet forward and grabs the prey with its large, sharp talons. If this blow does not kill the animal, the owl may give it a sharp bite at the base of the skull.

COUGH MIXTURE
Owls usually swallow their smaller prey whole, gulping down bones, fur, and feathers, as well as flesh. But they cannot digest these parts of their victims, so they cough them up again in the form of large pellets. By looking at the contents of an owl pellet, you can tell what the bird has eaten.

Large, strong wings make this owl a powerful flier.

There is a thick covering of soft feathers on the front of the body to keep the owl warm.

The large feet end in needle-sharp, curved talons for grasping and killing prey.

Feathers down to the toes help protect the owl from the bites of its prey.

OAK BUSH CRICKETS

DURING THE long summer days, oak bush crickets hide away among the forest leaves. They come out at night to feed on plants and small insects, or to search for a mate. The male attracts a female by making drumming or scraping sounds. After mating, the female lays her eggs in the soil, inside plant stems, or beneath the bark of a tree. She uses her sharp egg-laying tube, called an ovipositor, to carve a separate space for each egg. The young crickets, called nymphs, hatch the following spring. They look like miniature adults, but they have no wings. Their skin is hard and will not stretch, so in order to grow, they molt their skin several times to reveal a new one underneath. By late summer, each nymph has molted up to five times. After the final molt it has become a fully grown adult with wings.

FANTASTIC FEELERS
Oak bush crickets are sometimes called long-horned grasshoppers, because of their long, threadlike antennae. These help the cricket feel its way around in the dark. If the antennae sense an enemy ahead, their length gives the cricket a few extra inches to make its escape.

The large compound eyes can detect movement in almost every direction at the same time.

The bush cricket's ears are on its front legs, just below the knee joints.

A sharp claw on the end of each leg helps the insect grip on to plants.

FACT FILE
Name Oak bush cricket
(Meconema thalassinum)
Size 0.6 in (1.6 cm) long
Distribution Europe and Western Asia

LEAFY LOOK-ALIKE
The oak bush cricket blends in well with its leafy green surroundings. Its body is a similar color to the bushes where it lives, and its wings look like leaves. It is difficult for enemies, such as birds, to tell which is a leaf and which is a cricket.

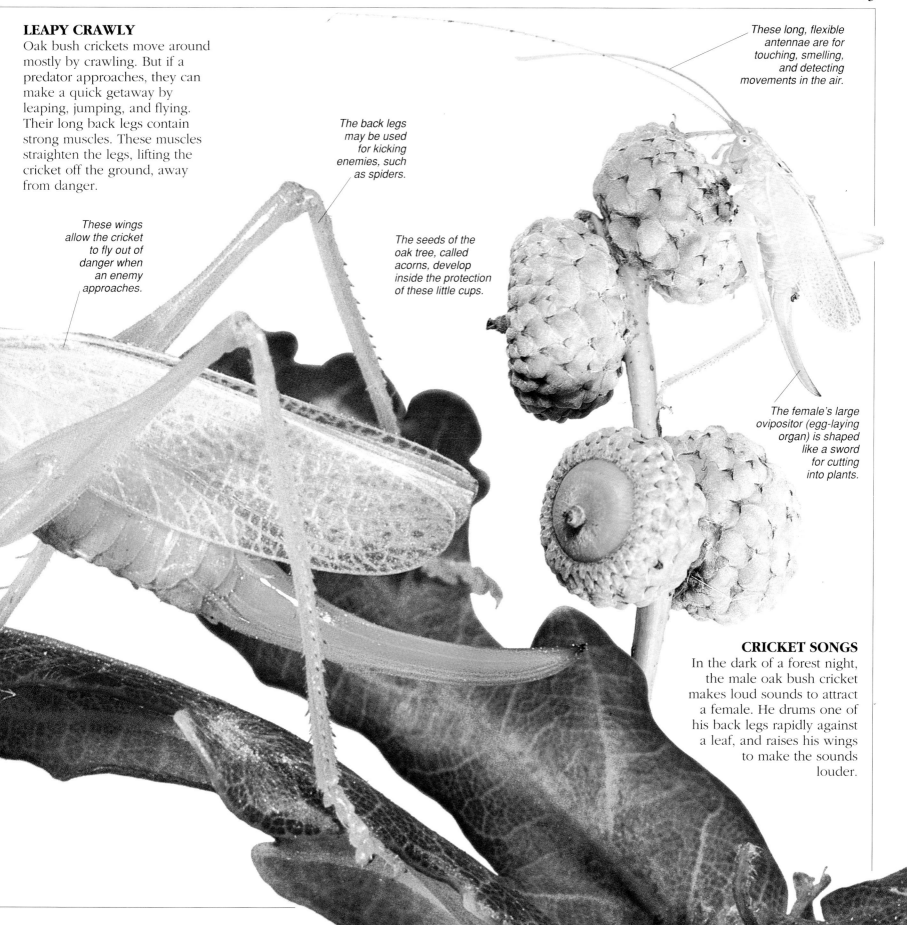

LEAPY CRAWLY
Oak bush crickets move around mostly by crawling. But if a predator approaches, they can make a quick getaway by leaping, jumping, and flying. Their long back legs contain strong muscles. These muscles straighten the legs, lifting the cricket off the ground, away from danger.

These long, flexible antennae are for touching, smelling, and detecting movements in the air.

The back legs may be used for kicking enemies, such as spiders.

These wings allow the cricket to fly out of danger when an enemy approaches.

The seeds of the oak tree, called acorns, develop inside the protection of these little cups.

The female's large ovipositor (egg-laying organ) is shaped like a sword for cutting into plants.

CRICKET SONGS
In the dark of a forest night, the male oak bush cricket makes loud sounds to attract a female. He drums one of his back legs rapidly against a leaf, and raises his wings to make the sounds louder.

FABULOUS FUNGI

LIKE LITTLE UMBRELLAS, toadstools sprout from tree trunks, branches, and leaf litter on the forest floor. Mushrooms and toadstools belong to a group of organisms called fungi. Fungi feed on plants and animals, both living and dead, whereas most plants make their food from air, water, and minerals. The main part of the fungus is hidden away inside whatever it is living on, such as a tree. It is made of a network of fine, branching threads, called hyphae. These are grouped together in a cobweblike net, called a mycelium. When a fungus is ready to reproduce, it forms fruit bodies, such as toadstools, above the surface. These can be all sorts of shapes, depending on the kind of fungus. Each fruit body contains millions of tiny spores, which are blown away by the wind, or carried off by animals that like to feed on the fungus. If the spores land in a suitable spot, they grow into new fungi.

These frills are found on many kinds of fungi. They are called gills, because they look like the gills of a fish.

RECYCLING EXPERTS

Without fungi, a forest would soon be buried under piles of dead leaves and other plant and animal remains. As the fungi feed on this dead and decaying material, they release some of the nutrients back into the soil. Plants take up these nutrients through their roots as they grow. So the fungi recycle materials that can be used over and over again.

This fungus is called slippery jack. Its name comes from the slimy covering on its cap. It grows beneath conifers, such as Scotch pine trees.

This ring shows where the cap used to be joined to the stalk while the fruit body was developing.

The spores are produced in masses of fine tubes under the cap.

At first, the fly agaric fungus is round, white, and egg-like. Then it grows a stalk with a rounded cap. Finally it develops into a flat-capped toadstool with a dip in the middle.

FACT FILE
Name Many-zoned fungi
(*Coriolus versicolor*)
Fly agaric
(*Amanita muscaria*)
Brown roll-rim
(*Paxillus involutus*)
Slippery jack
(*Suillus luteus*)

FLY KILLER

The bright red, poisonous fly agaric often lives on the roots of birch trees. The tree makes sugars that it stores in its roots, and the fungus takes some of these sugars to feed on. In return, the fly agaric helps the tree take up minerals from the soil, so both the tree and the fungus benefit from living together. Fly agaric gets its name from its use as a fly killer. People used to mix it with milk and sugar to make a sweet but deadly liquid, which flies loved to drink.

TRUNK TROUBLE

Some fungi produce fruit bodies that are shaped like shelf brackets. This is why they are called bracket fungi. These fungi often grow out of living tree trunks. In most cases, they eventually kill the tree. Other kinds of bracket fungi, like this many-zoned fungus, grow on dead tree stumps and fallen logs.

These white spots are the remains of the skin that covered the growing toadstool. They may be washed off by heavy rain.

This poisonous brown roll-rim is a good example of a funnel-shaped toadstool.

This kind of bracket fungus is called many-zoned, because it has different bands of color.

Frilly gills run down the stem of the brown roll-rim fungus. The spores fall from the edges of the gills.

Many-zoned fungus grows throughout the year on all kinds of dead wood.

HANDY ANTS

THESE WOOD ANTS live in enormous groups, called colonies, in nests at the base of coniferous trees. The nests are built by wingless females, called worker ants. Above ground is a mound up to nine feet across, made of conifer needles, dry grass, and tiny twigs. Below ground is a maze of chambers and tunnels. The queen is usually the only adult female with wings, and the only female to lay eggs. She lays her eggs deep within the nest. Workers care for the young during the egg and larval stages until they become young adults. Most of the eggs develop into workers, but some become males or new queens. On a warm, damp day in summer, swarms of young males and queens from all the nearby colonies fly high into the air to mate. The male ants die soon after mating, but the fertilized queens then start up new colonies.

Wood ants bite their enemies with these sharp mandibles (jaws), and squirt acid from their abdomen into the wound.

Joints allow the legs to bend, so the ant can climb and run.

The narrow waist makes the body very flexible.

These compound eyes are made up of many tiny lenses that see a pattern of light and dark dots.

FOOD FARMS

In the treetops, tiny aphids feed on a liquid called sap, which they suck from the leaves. The sap is partly digested by the aphids, then it oozes out of their rear ends as a sweet liquid called honeydew. Wood ants like to feed on honeydew, and they squeeze it out of aphids by stroking them with their antennae. Ants like honeydew so much that they carry about 600 pounds of it back to their nest every summer.

Claws help the ant grip on to surfaces when it is climbing.

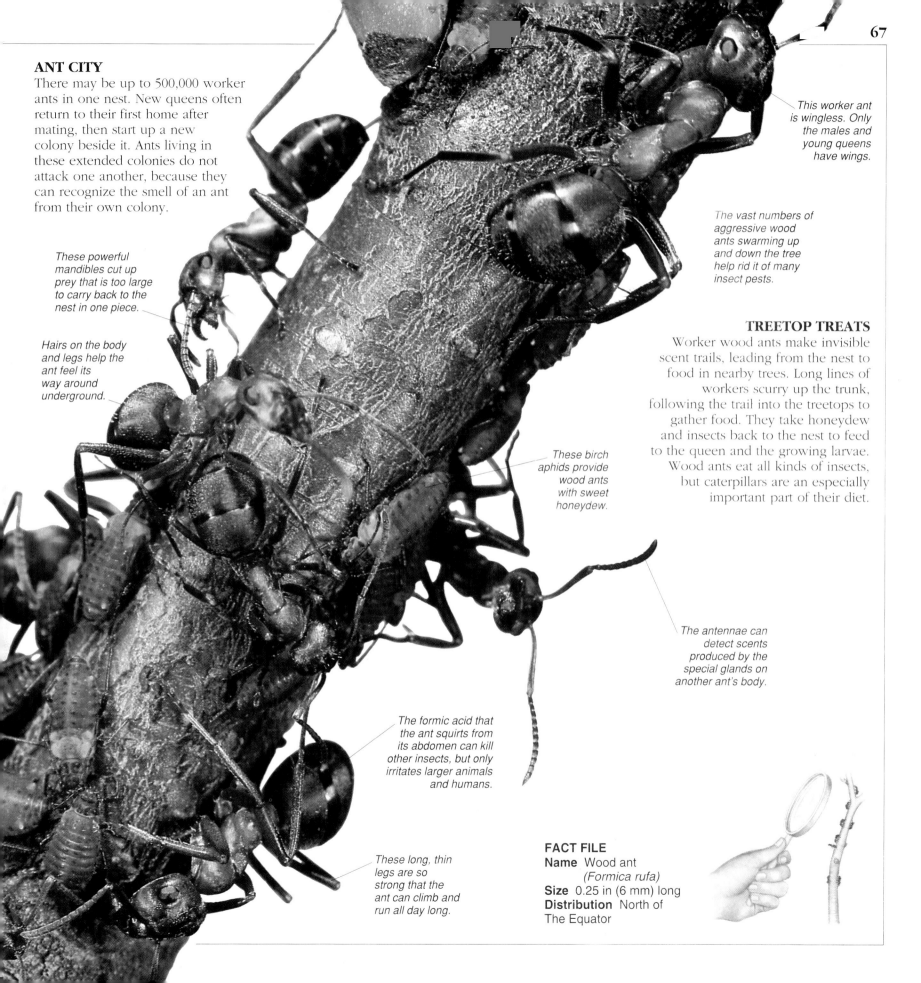

ANT CITY

There may be up to 500,000 worker ants in one nest. New queens often return to their first home after mating, then start up a new colony beside it. Ants living in these extended colonies do not attack one another, because they can recognize the smell of an ant from their own colony.

This worker ant is wingless. Only the males and young queens have wings.

The vast numbers of aggressive wood ants swarming up and down the tree help rid it of many insect pests.

These powerful mandibles cut up prey that is too large to carry back to the nest in one piece.

Hairs on the body and legs help the ant feel its way around underground.

TREETOP TREATS

Worker wood ants make invisible scent trails, leading from the nest to food in nearby trees. Long lines of workers scurry up the trunk, following the trail into the treetops to gather food. They take honeydew and insects back to the nest to feed to the queen and the growing larvae. Wood ants eat all kinds of insects, but caterpillars are an especially important part of their diet.

These birch aphids provide wood ants with sweet honeydew.

The antennae can detect scents produced by the special glands on another ant's body.

The formic acid that the ant squirts from its abdomen can kill other insects, but only irritates larger animals and humans.

These long, thin legs are so strong that the ant can climb and run all day long.

FACT FILE
Name Wood ant
(Formica rufa)
Size 0.25 in (6 mm) long
Distribution North of
The Equator

LAUGHING WOODPECKER

THE GREEN WOODPECKER'S loud, laughing call is unmistakable. You will often hear this bird long before you can see it. When it appears, in a flash of green, red, and yellow, the green woodpecker is instantly recognizable. It spends much of its time in among the trees, especially those on the edge of meadows and parks. It also comes down to the ground to look for insects, berries, and seeds to eat. The green woodpecker spends most of its life on its own. In spring, however, it pairs up with a mate. It builds its nest in a hole in a tree, and usually lays between five and seven eggs. Both parents incubate the eggs (keep them warm), and look after the young, called nestlings, once they have hatched.

CLEVER CLIMBER
The green woodpecker climbs up a tree trunk in jerky hops. Each foot has four toes ending in sharp, powerful claws. These help the woodpecker get a firm grip on the bark. Holding on tightly with its feet, the bird balances itself with its short, stiff tail.

TREE HOUSE
When it is time to build a nest, the green woodpecker chooses a tree where it can chip the wood away easily, such as a decaying oak or pine tree. The male and female take turns hammering away at the wood. The entrance to the nest hole is usually only about 3 in. wide, but inside it is much wider and about 12 in. deep, so there is plenty of room.

The tail is short and is made of stiff feathers which support the woodpecker as it climbs.

These bright green beech leaves have just unfurled from their protective cases.

NO HEADACHES

When the woodpecker hammers at wood with its beak, strong vibrations (movements) pass up the beak and into the head. To absorb these vibrations and protect the brain, there is a special layer between the bones of the beak and the rest of the head bones. This layer is made of a flexible, rubbery substance, called cartilage. For added protection, the front part of the skull is extra hard.

STICKY LICKER

The green woodpecker has an incredibly long tongue that can stick out of its beak by as much as 2 in. The tip of the tongue is covered with lots of sticky saliva. When the woodpecker pokes its tongue into an ant's nest, or into holes in rotten wood, any insects inside get stuck fast.

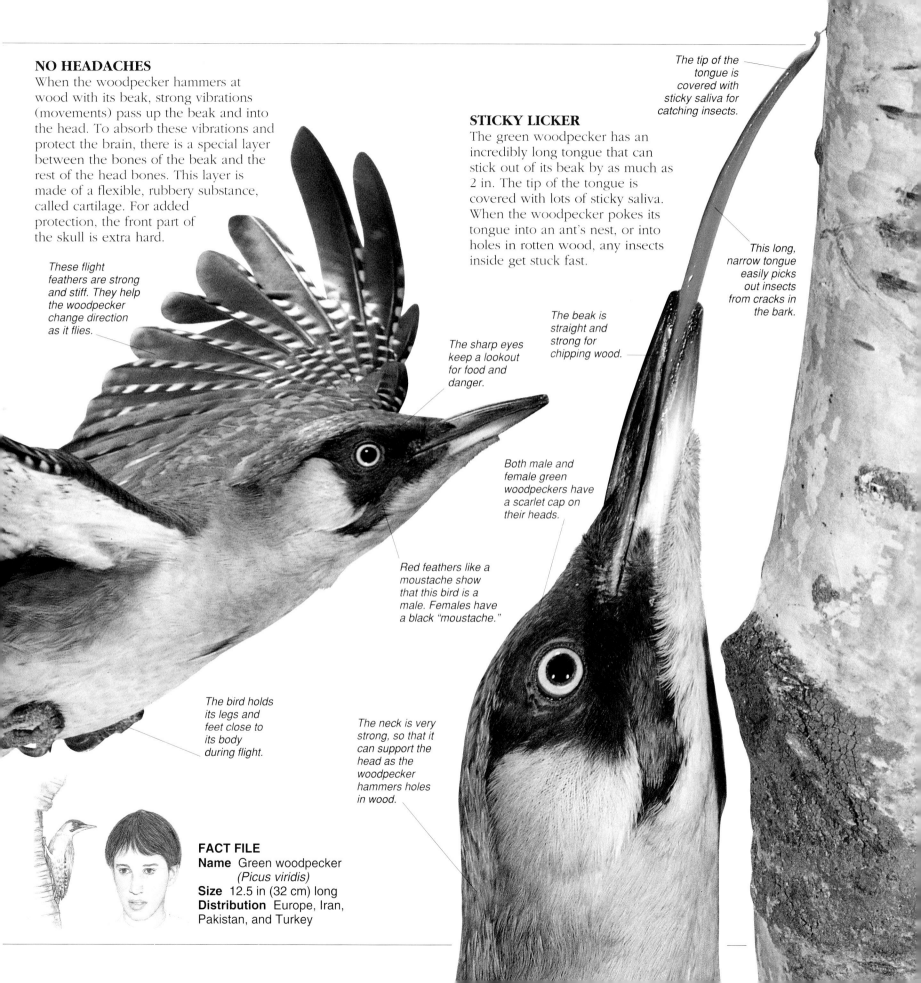

The tip of the tongue is covered with sticky saliva for catching insects.

This long, narrow tongue easily picks out insects from cracks in the bark.

The beak is straight and strong for chipping wood.

These flight feathers are strong and stiff. They help the woodpecker change direction as it flies.

The sharp eyes keep a lookout for food and danger.

Both male and female green woodpeckers have a scarlet cap on their heads.

Red feathers like a moustache show that this bird is a male. Females have a black "moustache."

The bird holds its legs and feet close to its body during flight.

The neck is very strong, so that it can support the head as the woodpecker hammers holes in wood.

FACT FILE
Name Green woodpecker
(*Picus viridis*)
Size 12.5 in (32 cm) long
Distribution Europe, Iran, Pakistan, and Turkey

DRILLER WASPS

ON SUNNY SUMMER days, male giant wood wasps fly around the treetops looking for a mate. Meanwhile, the females search for coniferous trees to lay their eggs in. After mating, each female drills narrow tunnels deep inside a tree using her long ovipositor. Then she lays one egg inside each hole. The females usually choose dead or dying trees, because the wood is softer for boring holes in. Two or three days later, caterpillarlike larvae hatch, and begin to chew away at the wood. Each larva grows very slowly because wood is hard to digest, and is not very nutritious. About two years later the larva starts to burrow its way out of the tree, stopping just below the surface. Then it spins a cocoon made of silk and bits of chewed wood. After several months, the cocoon splits and the adult wasp climbs out. It gnaws a short tunnel to escape, then flies off to find a mate.

FACT FILE
Name Giant wood wasp
(*Urocerus gigas*)
Size 1 in (2.5 cm) long
Distribution Asia, Europe, and Northern Africa

STRIPY TRICKS
Wasps and bees that can sting often have bright yellow and black stripes. These colors warn enemies that they are dangerous, and should be left alone. Giant wood wasps cannot sting, but they have similar striped coloring. This may fool enemies into thinking that they are dangerous.

The long, thin antennae are for feeling and smelling.

The compound eyes are made up of lots of lenses that build a complete picture, like a jigsaw.

Sensitive hairs pick up information about the surroundings.

Two pairs of delicate, transparent wings are supported by stiff veins.

HARMLESS HORNTAIL
Giant wood wasps are sometimes called horntails, because of the sharp spike at the end of the female's abdomen (rear part of the body). Below this spike is the long egg-laying tube, called the ovipositor. This ovipositor looks much like a fearsome stinger, but in fact it is quite harmless.

The thin legs are made up of several segments. They can bend at the joints.

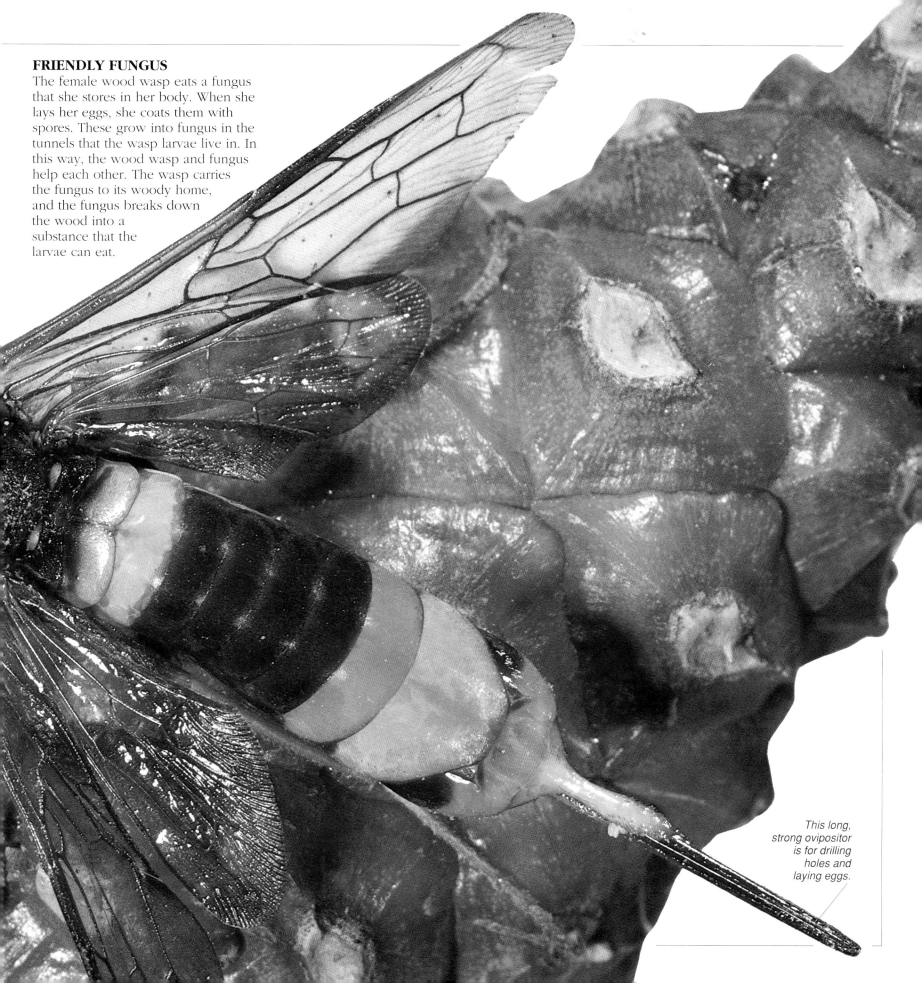

FRIENDLY FUNGUS
The female wood wasp eats a fungus that she stores in her body. When she lays her eggs, she coats them with spores. These grow into fungus in the tunnels that the wasp larvae live in. In this way, the wood wasp and fungus help each other. The wasp carries the fungus to its woody home, and the fungus breaks down the wood into a substance that the larvae can eat.

This long, strong ovipositor is for drilling holes and laying eggs.

PUSS MOTH CATERPILLARS

THESE LARGE, JUICY puss moth caterpillars are tasty treats for birds. So in order to protect themselves from attack, they put on a threatening display that tricks birds into thinking the caterpillars are much larger than they really are. The puss moth caterpillar is the feeding and growing stage in the life cycle of a puss moth. In early autumn, it finds a suitable place on a tree trunk and prepares to pupate. The caterpillar makes a case, called a cocoon, with silk from a special organ called a spinneret. It mixes the silk with chewed-up fragments of bark. This disguises the case, to protect the insect during the winter. By spring, the caterpillar has completely changed shape, and has become a winged adult moth. It produces a chemical that softens the tough cocoon, then cuts its way out and flies off to begin its life in the air.

KEEP YOUR DISTANCE

If an enemy approaches the puss moth caterpillar, a surprise is in store. The caterpillar suddenly draws its head back into its body, revealing a vivid red circle with two black spots that look like large eyes. At the same time, the two tails flick forward, and a fine red thread whips out from each. If this does not scare off the enemy, the caterpillar rears up and squirts out stinging formic acid from a special gland beneath its head.

FACT FILE
Name Puss moth caterpillar
(*Cerura vinula*)
Size 2.5 in (6 cm) long
Distribution Asia, Europe, and North Africa

Red threads shoot out from these tails to scare off enemies.

FAST FOOD

On warm spring nights, adult puss moths fly around trees, looking for a mate. The female moth lays up to three eggs at a time on the upper surface of the leaves. She usually lays them on more than one tree. This insures that each caterpillar has enough food to eat without having to go far.

The sharp mandibles are for cutting and chewing leaves.

These sharp barbs on the tails discourage enemies from eating the caterpillar.

Close up, you can see tiny holes, called spiracles, along the sides of the body. The caterpillar breathes through these holes.

TINY TOT

When the tiny larva first hatches, it is completely black with two little tails. Its tough, protective skin will not stretch, so in order to get bigger, the caterpillar grows a new skin underneath the old one, which it sheds. Caterpillars usually molt five or six times before they are fully grown.

These simple legs are for walking and holding on to twigs and leaves.

Rows of tiny hooks give a firm grip.

The body is divided up into segments, so it can bend.

The pattern on the caterpillar's body helps it hide among branches and leaves.

The caterpillar displays this bright red patch when it is threatened.

From the front, these eyespots look like the eyes of a much larger animal.

The caterpillar draws its head back into the thorax to reveal the eyespots.

The short antennae can tell which leaves are good to eat by their smell.

These true legs have special hooks for gripping food.

SUPER SWOOPERS

EASTERN ROSELLAS swoop through the trees, making bright splashes of color against the foliage. They call to other rosellas to let them know when they have found something to eat, and they screech to warn of danger. Eastern rosellas live in pairs or in small groups. In spring, the male puts on a dramatic performance to attract a mate. He droops his wings, fluffs up his breast feathers, and moves his fanned-out tail from side to side. After a male and female have mated, they usually stay together for the rest of their lives. They find a hole in a eucalyptus tree, where the female lays between four and seven white eggs. The male brings food for the female while she sits on the eggs to keep them warm. After the eggs have hatched, the parents look after their young until they are old enough to fly off on their own.

Sharp, beady eyes spot food easily.

The two outer toes point backward and the two inner toes point forward. This gives a strong hold on twigs and branches.

The rosella's beak never stops growing. If it did, the bird would soon wear it out, cracking seeds.

These sharp claws hold on tightly.

The flight feathers are strong and flexible, so they will not snap when the rosella flaps its wings.

The feathers overlap, so the body is a streamlined shape for flying fast.

HOOKING UP

Rosellas' toes curl around branches with a powerful, vice-like grip. Their long claws also help them get a firm hold, especially on smooth or slippery surfaces. When a rosella climbs up a tree, it hooks its beak around branches to pull itself upward.

HELPFUL HINGES

The rosella's short, thick beak is not firmly attached to its skull. Instead, both parts are hinged, so that they can move separately from the head. This makes it easier for the rosella to grasp and hold food.

The rosella spreads out its tail for support as it climbs.

FRUIT AND NUT
This rosella feeds mainly on seeds. It uses its strong beak like a nutcracker to break them open. Then it pulls out the kernel with its thick, knobby tongue. The rosella also eats fruit, nectar, and insects. To eat a piece of fruit, it makes a hole in the skin with its sharp beak. Then it scoops out the soft flesh inside the fruit.

There are nostrils on top of the beak for smelling food.

The beak is made of keratin, just like your fingernails.

Male rosellas like this one show off their brightly colored feathers to attract a mate.

FACT FILE
Name Eastern rosella
(*Platycercus eximius*)
Size 13 in (34 cm) long
Distribution Australia

INDEX

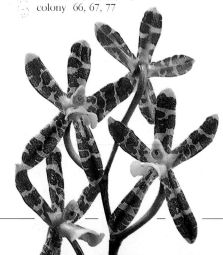

GLOSSARY

Abdomen *the rear of the body (in invertebrates)*
Acorn *the nut or fruit of an oak tree*
Amphibian *an animal that lives on land and in water*
Antennae *a pair of feelers*
Aphid *an insect that sucks sap from plants*
Aquatic *living or growing in or on water*

Boreal *living in the Northern Hemisphere*
Bromeliad *any plant of the family* Bromeliaceae, *which are often epiphytes*

Canopy *the highest level of branches and leaves, forming a rooflike covering*
Capsule *a kind of seed pod*
Carnivore *meat-eating animal*
Cartilage *the flexible, rubbery substance found between bones*
Chitin *the strong substance that makes up an insect's exoskeleton*
Chrysalis *the pupal stage of a butterfly*
Clutch *a set of eggs laid at one time*
Cocoon *a bag that a larva makes from silk when it is ready to pupate*
Colony *a group of animals or plants of the same kind that live together*
Compound eye *an eye that consists of many tiny separate lenses*
Conifer *an evergreen tree with cones*
Coniferous *having cones*
Conservation *protection and management of natural resources and the environment*
Cuticle *the waterproof outer layer of an animal or plant*

Decaying *rotting or decomposing*
Deciduous *losing all leaves once a year*
Deforestation *the clearing away of trees*
Dewlap *a fold of loose skin that hangs below the throat of some animals*
Distribution *the area or location where an animal or plant is found*
Dorsal *at the back of an animal's body*
Drey *a squirrel's nest*

Ecosystem *different communities of animals and plants interacting with their surroundings to form a stable system*
Elytra *the hard front wings of beetles that cover and protect the hind wings*
Epiphyte *a plant that grows on another plant, but takes no nourishment from it*
Erosion *wearing away*
Exoskeleton *a tough outer body covering*

Fang *a large, pointed tooth*
Foliage *the green leaves of a plant*
Forest *an area with a dense growth of trees*

Forewing *a front wing*
Frond *the leaf of a fern*
Gills (in fish) *the organs that fish use to take in oxygen from water*
Gills (in fungi) *the spore-producing plates on the underside of a cap*
Gnaw *to bite or chew steadily*

Habitat *the natural home of an animal or plant*
Herbivore *a plant-eating animal*
Honeydew *plant sap that has passed through the body of an aphid*
Hyphae *the underground threads of a fungus*

Incisor *a sharp tooth at the front of the mouth*
Incubate *to provide eggs with heat for their development*

Keratin *the protein in hair, fur, and nails*
Kernel *an inner seed or nut*

Labellum *part of an orchid flower*
Larva *a grub that eventually develops into an adult*
Latex *a milky sap found in some plants*
Lenticel *a pore in the stem of a plant*

Mammal *an animal that produces milk to feed its young, such as a squirrel*
Mandibles (in insects) *a pair of mouthparts for biting and chewing food*
Mangrove swamp *a tropical coastal forest, where mangrove trees grow in the shallow water*
Melanin *a pigment in hair, skin, or eyes*
Membrane *a thin elastic skin*
Metamorphosis *the change from a larva to an adult (in insects)*
Molt *to shed the skin or exoskeleton*
Mucus *a slimy, sometimes poisonous substance*
Mycelium *the mass of hyphae that makes up the body of a fungus*

Nectar *a sugary fluid produced by flowers*
Nutrient *a substance, such as a mineral, that plants and animals need in order to stay healthy*
Nymph *the larva of certain kinds of insects*

Organism *any living animal or plant*
Osteoderm *a bony plate in the skin, which gives animals extra protection*
Ovipositor *the egg-laying tube at the tip of the abdomen in most female insects*

Parasite *a plant or animal that lives in or on another living thing and takes nourishment from it*
Pedicel *the narrow part of a spider's body*
Pedipalp *the leglike part on a spider's head*
Pellet *undigested food regurgitated by an owl*
Photosynthesis *the use of sunlight by plants to produce the energy for growing*
Pigment *a substance that produces color in organisms*
Pollen *the fine dust produced by a flower's stamens*
Pollination *the transfer of pollen from the stamens to the stigma of a flower*
Predator *an animal that hunts other animals for food*
Preening *when a bird grooms its feathers with its beak*
Proleg *a fleshy, leglike structure without joints*
Pseudobulb *the stem of an orchid that swells with stored food and water like a bulb*
Pupa *an insect in the stage between larva and adult, enclosed in a case*

Pupate *to develop into a pupa*
Prehensile *able to grasp objects, for example, when a monkey uses its tail to hold onto a branch*
Proboscis *the strawlike mouthpart of a butterfly*

Rain forest *a forest found in an area of heavy rainfall*
Recycle *to use again*
Respiration *breathing*
Rhizome *a thick underground stem where food is stored in some plants*
Roost *to rest or sleep, often in a high place*

Saliva *a liquid that forms in the mouth*
Scale *a tough, platelike protective covering*
Sepal *the outer part of a flower that protects the bud*
Sloughing *the shedding of skin*
Spinneret *a tiny silkproducing organ in spiders and some insects*
Spiracle *the hole in an insect's exoskeleton through which it breathes*
Spore *a seed-like body produced by flowerless plants and simple animals*
Stamen *the male part of a flower, where the pollen is made*
Stigma *the female part of a flower, that receives pollen*
Stolon *a creeping overground stem that produces a new plant*
Streamlined *a shape that moves easily through air, water, or soil*
Style *the part of a flower that supports the stigma*

Talon *the sharp, hooked claw of a bird*
Temperate *moderate or mild in temperature*
Territory *an area that an animal occupies and defends*
Thorax (in invertebrates) *the middle part of the body containing the heart and lungs*
Toxic *poisonous*
Trachea *a windpipe for breathing*
Transparent *see-through*
Tubular *long and hollow*

Vibration *a tiny movement*

Woodland *land that is mostly covered with trees and shrubs*